The Writer's Life

Writer's Life Volume 1

Vincent Zandri

Published by Vincent Zandri, 2023.

Also by Vincent Zandri

A Chase Baker Thriller
Chase Baker and the Spear of Destiny

A Chase Baker Thriller No. 12
Chase Baker and the Lost Ark of God

A Chase Baker Thriller Series No. 3
Chase Baker and the God Boy

A Chase Baker Thriller Series No. 4
Chase Baker and the Lincoln Curse

A Chase Baker Thriller Series No. 6
Chase Baker and the Da Vinci Divinity

A Dick Moonlight PI Series
Moonlight Falls
Blue Moonlight
Moonlight Weeps

A Dick Moonlight PI Series Short
Moonlight Goes Viral
Moonlight Mafia
Moonlight Detour

A Dick Moonlight PI Thriller
Moonlight Falls: New and Lengthened Editor's Cut Edition

A Dick Moonlight Thriller Book 9
Dog Day Moonlight

A Gripping Ava "Spike" Harrison Thriller
The Concrete Pearl

A Gripping Dick Moonlight PI Thriller
Moonlight Sonata

A Gripping Tanya Teal Corporate War Chronicles Thriller
Primary Termination

A Jack "Keeper" Marconi PI Thriller Series
The Innocent
American Prison Break
The Jack "Keeper" Marconi PI Box Set

(A Keeper Marconi PI Thriller Book 5
Dressed to Kill

A Meta Man Time Travel Thriller
Meta Man
Meta Man: Mars 900 C
Cashless Bail
After Life

A Sam Savage Sky Marshal Thriller
Dead Heading
Tunnel Rats

A Short Thriller
Ghosts

Pembroke PInes
The Devil Won't Have You
The Girl in the Window
Go Get Me A Gun
The Left Hook
Autonomous
Delusional
Desperate Measures
Domestic Dispute
Living Doll

A Short Thriller Collection
Desperate Measures: A Short Thriller Collection

A Short True Crime Thriller
I Am God

A Steve Jobz PI Thriller
The Flower Man
The Extortionist

A Steve Jobz Thriller
The Embalmer

(A Thriller)

The Scream Catcher
Detonator

A Vincent Zandri Hard-Boiled Short Read
Bingo Night
Pathological

PULP Thrillers
Pulp 2: Three Gripping Thrillers Collected in One Box Set

The Handyman
Savage Sins: The Handyman, Season II, Episode III

The Handyman Season I, Episode I
Lust and Letters

(Vincent Zandri on Writing Book)
Pieces of Mind: Fictional Truths & Non-Fictional Lies about Writing
and the Writing Life

Writer's Life Volume 1
The Writer's Life

Standalone
Head
Pathological: Collected Short Reads of Sex, Lies, and Murder!
Go Get Me a Gun

Watch for more at https://www.vinzandri.com/.

PRAISE FOR VINCENT ZANDRI

Grab a FREE thriller at www.vinzandri.com[1]

"Sensational . . . masterful . . . brilliant."

—New York Post

"(A) chilling tale of obsessive love from Thriller Award–winner Zandri (Moonlight Weeps) . . . Riveting."

—Publishers Weekly

". . . Oh, what a story it is . . . Riveting . . . A terrific old school thriller."

—Booklist "Starred Review"

"Zandri does a fantastic job with this story. Not only does he scare the reader, but the horror

Show he presents also scares the man who is the definition of the word "tough."

—Suspense Magazine

---

1. *http://www.vinzandri.com*

"I very highly recommend this book . . . It's a great crime drama that is full of action and intense suspense, along with some great twists . . . Vincent Zandri has become a huge name and just keeps pouring out one best seller after another."

—Life in Review

"(The Innocent) is a thriller that has depth and substance, wickedness and compassion."

—The Times-Union (Albany)

"The action never wanes."

—Fort Lauderdale Sun-Sentinel

"Gritty, fast-paced, lyrical and haunting."

—Harlan Coben, New York Times bestselling author of *Six Years*

"Tough, stylish, heartbreaking."

—Don Winslow, New York Times bestselling author of *SASHLEYges* and *Cartel.*

"A tightly crafted, smart, disturbing, elegantly crafted complex thriller . . . I dare you to start it and not keep reading."

—MJ Rose, New York Times bestselling author of *Halo Effect* and *Closure*

"A classic slice of raw pulp noir..."

—William Landay, New York Times bestselling author of *Defending Jacob*

The Writer's Life: Rants, Raves & Writings

Volume One

Vincent Zandri

"If my doctor told me I had only six minutes to live, I wouldn't brood. I'd type a little faster." Isaac Asimov

An Introductory Writing Rant

I came up with the notion of creating The Writer's Life YouTube channel about a year and a half ago now. Deep inside, I knew my career needed something more than I was giving it. That's not to say that I wasn't working harder than ever. It's just that I wasn't working smarter. In essence, I was sort of all over the place. Plus, I didn't know if I should continue working with so many publishers who seemed completely disinterested in pushing my books or concentrate mostly on my own publishing company, Bear Media.

It turns out, I chose the latter while still working with a publisher or two (I'm a hybrid author). Not only did I start the YouTube channel, but I began a Substack Newsletter which is yet another indie outlet, plus I started to write at Pulp Speed. That means I write anywhere between 2K and 3K consumable words per day, every day.

The plan was and remains, to publish rapidly, no matter what traditionally based publishing house I pissed off. I also promised myself that I would stick to this new plan and by the time I turned 62 years old (when I would be eligible for early Social Security; I'm 58 as of this writing), I would have at least 250 Intellectual Properties to my name which would be making me very decent money month after month after month. What's the golden rule when it comes to publishing? More books equate to more sales.

Notice I often utilize the term Intellectual Property in the place of books and stories. That's because IP is like owning tangible property, like a street corner in New York City for instance. If you keep up the property and continue to rent out the empty spaces and purchase more buildings with your profits, you will eventually be worth a few bucks. And so will your children and your children's children. When you give away your IP to a publisher, it's like giving away one of the apartments on your property for a single, small, one-time fee. Now, how stupid is that?

These days, I'm putting out new books and stories like crazy. There are very few professional writers who can keep up with my output. I'm also a freelance journalist and writer. Believe it or not, being a full-time writer is still a part-time gig. Go figure. I no longer depend on bookstores, agents, or traditional publishers to satisfy my neurotic need to see my name in print. In the words of James Altucher (who believes in indie publishing), I choose myself.

I have no problem pissing off the powers that be in the writing industry. In fact, it gives me great joy for them to know that it's me with all the power, not them. "It's not supposed to work that way," they think while grinding their teeth. "He's supposed to bow down before me and kiss my boots."

Yeah, well, kiss my ass.

I once was represented by arguably the best New York literary agent in NYC. I won't mention her name but her Christian name rhymes with "luck" and she was at the time, a big deal at the William Morris Agency. But it turns out, she was a failure. She couldn't sell one of my best efforts, Moonlight Falls, which would go on to sell to several publishers and today is in its fourth printing (I actually forget at this point). But that one failure on her part didn't entice her to want to do better next time.

It had the opposite effect.

She blamed me for her incompetence. From that point on, she wouldn't take my calls and if she did, she acted like a high school snot who just hooked up with a new boyfriend. Eventually, she passed me on to an associate agent who didn't know his ass from a hole in the ground.

It was their way of showing me the door and issuing me a cold, "Buh bye."

"Promise?" I whispered to myself with a grin.

I never looked back, nor will I ever.

Vincent Zandri

Albany, NY

March 25, 2023

P.S.: the writings in this book are presented exactly as I wrote and published them originally for other publications and platforms, warts and all. Find a typo? Deal with it.

1

Be Careful What You Wish For

The literal definition of the word confluence, thanks to Google (what would we do without Google?), is the place where two rivers merge. The image is just too rich to ignore as a metaphor, especially for full-time writers like me.

I have had times in my twenty-plus year career when I could do no wrong. I just happened to be writing the right manuscript (The Innocent), at the right time (the late 1990's), which I sent to the right agent (Jimmy Vines in NYC), who sold it to the right marketplace (Delacorte Press) in a two book, hard and soft deal worth $235K. I was floored.

Movie companies were frantically calling and full feature picture deals were being considered by the likes of Dreamworks and Robert DeNiro's production company. Even George Clooney wanted in. There were others, but I forget them now. But you get the point. Newspapers and magazines wanted to write about me and I happily sat for their interviews. I'm partying in New York City with my agent and editor, renting lavish hotel suites in Gramercy Park, and dining out in expensive steakhouses. I was maybe 33 years old. It was a magical time.

The novel, which is now renamed As Catch Can since another author had already used the title, is released to spectacular reviews. The New York Post writes me a love letter. They call it, "Sensational...masterful...brilliant." Says the Times Union, "As Catch Can is a thriller that has depth and substance, wickedness and compassion." Don Winslow calls it "...tough, stylish, heartbreaking."

Can this novel do no wrong?

The Writer's Curse: The Big Yawn

As it turns out, yes it can. Despite the great reviews and media attention, the novel doesn't sell. When it comes to book buyers, all we get is the big yawn. When I tell people I meet on the street or inside some bar, the title, As Catch Can, they inevitably look at me with furrowed brow and respond, "As Catch what?" Even when they finally get it, they search for a book called Catch As Catch Can, and I lose yet another sale. Things tumble downwards from there in a ... wait for it... confluence of disasters.

I've put the majority of my advance into a new house, while my wife at the time asks me for a divorce. Whatever money I have left, goes to the divorce lawyer and alimony payments (the divorce was ugly, but we're good friends now). I had been a freelancer prior to the big deal, but since I was falsely convinced more and more huge deals were right around the corner, I cut ties with my clients. My agent won't return my calls, my publisher won't publish anymore books once the contract is fulfilled, I owe the IRS a bunch of cash, and I'm out of work.

Getting a major deal might have been the worst thing to ever happen to me.

Damage Control for the Writer

Fast forward a few years. I'm in full damage control mode, and back to freelance writing, slowly digging myself out of my professional and financial hole. I'm also back to writing fiction on the side. I pen a new detective novel called Moonlight Falls and I sell it to a small press. Its not the biggest deal in the world, but I'm officially back in the game. I write another Dick Moonlight PI novel, Moonlight Rises, and then I write a big standalone called The Remains. It's at this time, a nifty little device called the eBook reader hits the marketplace and along with it, numerous publishing platforms. All sorts of little publishers are springing up. eBooks are their bread and butter.

In the meantime, my new agent has successfully gotten the rights to The Innocent (As Catch Can) and its follow-up, Godchild, back from Delacorte. It was a stroke of very good luck. Because what that meant was, I could now republish both books with my new publisher.

The Writer is Back on Top

I'm in Italy with my then girlfriend when more good news comes my way. The Innocent is not only rocketing up the charts, it will eventually land in the Number 2 spot on the overall, let's call it, Zon bestseller list and stay in the top ten for a full month. Altogether, I will sell 100K copies in a little more than 6 weeks. At the same time, Godchild will sell 25K copies. And my new novel, The Remains, will sell 25K+ copies also. The movie companies are calling again and so is the press. It's a confluence of good luck.

I'll go on to land another major deal with a major publisher for all of the above-stated novels, plus the entire Dick Moonlight PI series. I'll hit the New York Times and USA Today bestseller lists with a box set I'm included in, and my novel Moonlight Weeps will win both the ITW Thriller Award and the PWA Shamus Award. Suddenly, life is grand again.

A Golden Age Dawns for Genre Fiction Writers

Despite the good karma, I'm not as stupid as I was years earlier when I decided to live life like a rock star and give up creating opportunities for myself. Success in the writing business can be cyclical at best, fleeting at worst. That said, I start a small publishing company called Bear Media, and I begin publishing several brand-new series under its imprints. Books like The Shroud Key, sell tens of thousands of copies, others not so much, but they still sell, and I don't have to split the proceeds with another publisher or an agent. I can also write whatever the hell I want. Best of all, I have total control. I'm no longer a slave to the fickle publishing system. The golden age of genre fiction writing was upon us.

Not Everything is Rosy for the Writer

Spring ahead another few years. The editors and marketing pros I worked with at the major imprint are gone and a whole new crew has taken their place. I still have maybe five novels with them, including The Remains, but they rarely communicate with me anymore and my once four-figure per month income has dwindled considerably. But I now have forty-plus novels under my own label, and I'm writing new books for two more publishers. By the looks of things, I'm about to strike a contract extension with one of them. We're also getting movie interest again.

The point to all this? The older you get, the more you recognize the seesaw patterns in the professional writing business. To put it simply, nothing is guaranteed, and like I once told the New York Times in a 2014 interview, publishers aren't in the business to be your friend. One day they're wining and dining you, and the next they're ghosting your emails. A writer can go through years of total media disinterest and then suddenly, you're once more an overnight sensation.

The thing to keep in mind is this: the highs are never that high and the lows are really never that low. There are going to be good times, and you must learn to endure the bad by creating your own income streams like I did with Bear Media. That's the reality of the writer's life. But hey, that's show biz, folks. Don't like it? Get a real job.

2

A Case of the Mondays

The writing life isn't only about art, it's also about making a passive income. Because who wants to work a real job anyway?

Anyone who's ever watched the 1999 movie, Office Space, knows just how dreadful and soul sucking a day job can be. Being ball-and-chained to a small cubicle for eight and half hours per day is, to many people, a form of slavery. But hey, unless you're independently wealthy, everyone's got to work. We have to eat, right? We have bills to pay.

Too bad most Americans are said to be only $400 away from being flat broke, meaning, they not only live paycheck to paycheck, but they also can't afford it when their car breaks down or the refrigerator goes on the fritz. If that's not depressing enough, you're still expected to show up for work on Monday morning.

A Case of the Mondays

In Office Space, the main character Peter, played by actor Ron Livingston, is so depressed after having arrived at his dull, soul sucking job on a Monday morning, he decides to skip out for a coffee along with a couple coworkers. They visit a nearby cheesy chain establishment, Chotchkies, which is sort of like TGIF Fridays on steroids. Like Fridays, the staff is not only expected to where an obnoxious uniform covered in "flair," their attitude must be over-the-top happy.

The server assigned to Peter and his buddies is just one such individual. As they sit down, the server, Brian, played by actor, Todd Duffey, plants a broad, if not obnoxious smile on his face. It's a direct contrast to the gloomy, upside-down faces seated around the table.

"Sounds like a case of the Mondays," Happy Server Brian says.

I'm not going to give away too much of the movie's plot, but suffice to say, from that point on, Peter is determined to find a way not only to get rid of his job, which is presided over by his evil boss, William Lumbergh (Gary Cole), he wants to find a means of employment that will allow him to do nothing at all, every day, all day.

Maybe Peter didn't realize it at the time, but what he's talking about is passive income.

Writing as Passive Income

One of the main reasons I got into freelance writing and fiction writing in the first place was to avoid a day job. I was groomed to run an industrial and commercial construction company. Immediately after college, I was given a week off and told to report to the office. There was no backpacking in Europe with my friends, no heading to New York City to land a job perhaps as a cub reporter, no heading cross country to find my fortune on my own terms...no fun of any kind.

I was to report to the office and begin my apprenticeship as a junior executive. Here's how the first year went: I hated every minute of it. Now this is not to come down on what many people would consider the opportunity of a lifetime, and it was. But the problem was this: I knew in my bones the career wasn't for me. I couldn't stand being cooped up in an office all day checking packing slips and asking for quotes on windows and doors. It wasn't my cup of tea.

Emotionally speaking, here's how a typical week would go. Monday morning is a horrible experience exacerbated by lack of sleep, anxiety over what the day will bring, and the empty feeling of utter hopelessness since at that moment in time, another Friday seems like an impossible dream.

By Tuesday you loosen up a little and resign yourself to the job. By Wednesday you see the light at the end of the tunnel. Thursday you're starting to feel like you're gonna make it after all. Friday you're exuberant. Friday night you get drunk with your friends, and you do so again on Saturday. By Sunday the hangover kicks in and by Sunday night you're miserable once again because guess what day dawns in the morning?

Rediscovering Hemingway

In my spare time, I read all the books I couldn't read or didn't have the time to read during my undergraduate years. I was especially fond of the Hemingway novels and short stories. I also got heavily into the Hemingway biographies, especially the Carlos Baker biography which, at the time, was considered the quintessential work on the adventurous author.

I loved it.

I wasn't halfway through with the big book when I realized, this is the life for me. Hemingway didn't just write, he lived the life he was writing about. He lived in Paris, went to the bullfights in Spain, hunted lions in Africa, fished on the Gulf Stream, married a very rich lady, built a house in Key West, and what's more, he never had a real job other than a few short years as a full-time newspaperman.

The Hemingway life was the life I wanted to experience. When the realization sank in, it was like a big bright light had gone off inside my brain and my heart. I felt lighter than air because I had found my true calling. It must have been what a priest experiences when he finally discovers his sacred mission in life.

I didn't waste any time. That day I announced to all my friends that I was giving up the construction business to be a writer.

They all laughed at me.

Proving the Naysayers Wrong

Proving the naysayers wrong would not only take determination, it would take guts and a willingness to start at the bottom. After all, back then, I had more enthusiasm than talent. I started writing on the side. Taking a cue from the great Hemingway, I got a job at the local Times Union Newspaper writing sports stories on the weekends. I also started freelancing for them. Stories ranging from fly fishing for trout and bass, to travel pieces, to book reviews.

Again, like Hemingway, I tried my hand at writing some short stories. Before long I found myself getting published in journals like the Maryland Review, Fugue, Old Hickory Review, Buffalo Spree, Orange County Magazine and many more. My journalism was getting published in New York Newsday and Hudson Valley Magazine, and I would be accepted into the prestigious Bread Loaf Writers Conference in Vermont. I was working hard, but I was also making a little money and, more importantly, making my way as a literary neophyte.

That's when I applied to Vermont College for my MFA in Writing. I was accepted. Suddenly, my friends were no longer laughing at me.

Back to a Case of the Mondays

There was no stopping me. I plowed through writing school like a man possessed and, in the process, sold a novel that would fetch a very major deal. And while that deal would have its issues, I would never again work a real job.

That was over twenty years ago.

The writing life has had plenty of ups and downs since then, but I can still wake up on Monday mornings, and if I so choose, roll over and go back to sleep. What's more, I can do this in Italy if I want, as easily as I can do it here in New York. Books sales, for the most part, are a passive income monster. You sell books while you're sleeping or, like Peter from Office Space aspires to, while you're doing absolutely nothing at all.

Come to think of it, I've worked really hard for the right to do nothing.

3

Why I Never Get Writer's Block

Last evening, I spoke with one of my publishers about the new book I was writing. Without hesitation, he penciled in a possible publication date for late 2020 or early 2021. He did this without even reading a single word of the book. He did this without having to honor a contract, since we don't have a contract yet. I'll leave that up to my agent to discuss with him. When I further revealed, I have enough material...enough new books...to carry me well into 2023, he told me I'm a writing machine.

"Don't you ever get writer's block?" he asked.

"Never," I said. "My dad never got construction workers block and he died with his boots on. I plan to do the same."

Proliferation

I'm not sure if the gift for proliferation is something you're born with, or something that's learned. What's for sure, if I've always had a habit of writing a lot of words, even when I was still learning the trade (I drove my writing professors totally insane). This is not to say, my books and stories are long winded. Quite the opposite, in fact. I shoot for short, sharp declarative sentences. I keep the description to a minimum. Few adjectives, almost no adverbs. Nothing frilly. It just means I can write a lot of stories in a short amount of time, when other writers struggle even to come up with ideas.

Writing in the Dark

I'm not sure who coined the phrase, writing in the dark. Perhaps it was Dean Wesley Smith, another extremely prolific genre writer. All he needs is to start with a title, and he can sit down and begin a new story or novel without even knowing what the plot is about. Now that's professionalism.

Glory Days of Pulp Magazines

Back in the glory days of the pulps in the 1930s, 40s, and 50s, a writer like me could make great money writing mysteries and adventures for a penny a word. Back then, you wrote on real typewriters, and you had no choice but to write clean copy. All it took was discipline and time in the writing chair. It also took talent. But more importantly, it took something else. Love of the craft.

If you don't love what you're writing, it's going to show up on the page, glaringly. The reader will get bored, put the book down, and likely, never read another one of your stories again.

Treat the Writing like a Job

Much like the pulp era of yesteryear, we are presently in the midst of a golden age of genre fiction. People will gladly pay for good content (writers are no longer considered writers but instead, content specialists). Good being the key word. So, I wish to leave you with a trick of the trade that has always worked for me.

Tomorrow morning, get your butt out of bed early. Even if it's cold, gloomy, and rainy. Get out of bed, make the coffee, and sit yourself down at your writing desk. Only, here's the thing: pretend you're not writing in your pajamas inside your bedroom. Convince yourself the Disney Studio or Paramount Productions has hired you to write 2,000 new words a days, every day, five days per week (they want you to do 1,000 words on Saturday). You don't produce 2,000 new, very good words per day, you don't get paid. Even worse, there's some young, snot nosed kid standing just outside the door waiting to take your place.

I have to end this piece here, because I need to write another story before lunchtime. I have no idea what I'm going to write about.

4

How to Write a Novel in 30 Days (With Time to Spare)

Yes, it's possible to write a novel in 30 days and still have lots of time left on your hands. You just need to be disciplined.

You hear all the time about the writers who take, or took, years to write a single, 60K word novel. They sweated over every single word, toiled over every sentence, lost sleep over every paragraph, only to toss the whole damn thing out in the end. This is a sad state of affairs during any era, but in this, the new golden age of fiction writing, it is downright tragic.

The Need for Proliferation

Readers...serious serial readers...crave content. I'm talking the readers who can devour a book or sometimes two books per day. These are the special people writers like me are targeting. The readers who will read my books as fast as me and my various publishers can put them out. Relatively speaking, there aren't that many serial readers out there, but all you need is a fraction of them who read (or listen in the case of audio books) all your stuff in order to make a very nice living.

The Need to Write Fast

Proliferation not only takes talent, it takes speed. But speed, my friends, is relative. I know authors who are penning not one book per month, but two and even three, plus writing blogs and articles in their spare time. Many of these authors have families and perhaps part-time jobs.

So where do they find the time to write so many books? They don't find the time. They make the time.

How to Write a Novel in 30 Days

Time for some math (or maths as the Brits like to say). A single, double-spaced page of copy contains approximately 250 words. Four of those pages will get you 1,000 words. First thing I do when I wake up in the morning, is grab the coffee, sit down and write about 1,000 new words on average, meaning sometimes it's 750 words, and other times, 1250. But you get the point.

The writing session usually takes me an hour to an hour and a half. I take little breaks in between to heat up my coffee, or just go outside and breathe the fresh air. When that hour and a half session is done, I go for a short run and lift some weights. That also takes me about an hour and a half. After that, I'll shower up, and sit back down at my desk where I'll write maybe another 500 words. This takes me into lunch time.

Lunch is usually enjoyed at my desk, where I'll write another 250 to 500 words. When that's done, I like to break for a quick nap. The nap is essential in that I feel like a brand-new man when it's done (I don't really sleep. It's more like entering into a meditative state). Back at my desk with a cup of coffee by my side, I will either complete my 2,000 words, or if they are already done, I might write a few more just to get ahead so that perhaps I can take Sunday off. Or, I'll edit the words I've already written along the way.

Speaking of the editing process...

Edit as You Go

For me, writing a novel in a month's time requires that I edit my words as I write them. This provides me with two advantages over those who simply plow through a first draft. It not only allows me to write semi-error free, tight sentences the first time around, it also keeps my literary train on the tracks, rather than veer off the rails into a place my story has no business of going.

Which leads me to...

Outline as You Go

I'm not necessarily a pantser nor do I rely on detailed outlines. This is art after all, and art has a way of taking over and going where it will if you don't reign it in, within reason that is (see the above metaphor about going off the rails). But like Hemingway once said, what's the best way to ensure that come the next morning, you'll be able to carry on with your story? It's by knowing what's going to happen next.

That said, not only do I stop for the day in a place where I know what's going to happen next, I outline along the way by jotting down two or three story points that will keep the narrative flowing come the following morning. Do that consistently and you will never ever have to worry about writer's block again.

And in The End

If you've stuck to your 2,000 word per day schedule. If you've been disciplined enough to edit what you've written every single day, if you've outlined along the way, then by day 30 (or perhaps even sooner), you will have completed your novel.

5

Proliferation to Profit: A Lesson Learned

Do you write only when you feel like writing? Perhaps you consider yourself a hobbyist and you don't much care about making a profit from your words. It could be that you have a day job, preferably one you like, and you don't need the money that can potentially come from your writing. If that's the case, may you go with God and prosper.

But what about the rest of us who write for a living, be it as a freelance writer, journalist, blogger, nonfiction book author, fiction book author, or a rather strange and stressful all-of-the-above combination? We have no choice but to profit from our words, one by bloody one, or else the rent doesn't get paid...The food doesn't get served...The car gets repossessed. The words stop flowing, the cash stops coming in. What's the only choice you have left? Getting the dreaded day job.

I'd rather hang from the ceiling by my nipples.

Writing School

In writing school, I wrote far more material than was required by my professors. I wrote so many words, I drove some of them nuts. But when I told them that I planned on making a career out of my writing...that I planned on "entertaining" readers...I was only derided, and laughed at behind my back when the professors returned to their dorms for the evening. Well, laugh it up, because while you're still teaching the same thing over and over again, year after year, I've sold hundreds of thousands of books and made close to a million bucks in the past ten years alone. And I'm not even close to being as popular an author as say the Dan Browns of the world, or even uber-successful indie authors like Hugh Howey or JR Rain.

The Value of the Written Word: Pay the Writer

Words should be exchanged for cold hard cash. I'm a staunch believer that if your words get printed, you should be paid for them. Sadly, we no longer get paid for everything we write. With the advent of the Internet, our words have become democratized. Blogs like this one are all the rage, but so are YouTube videos, Tweets, Facebook Posts, and more. I've even written for some stellar publications that no longer pay (they shall go unnamed). Payment, they say, is exposure, or perhaps the reader will pay indirectly by buying one of my books. I find this appalling on one hand, but reality on the other.

Writers have always had to beg and grovel to get ahead. Why should that change now?

Proliferation

What's a writer to do? Quite simply, write. I'm not necessarily a speed demon at the typewriter, but I can easily write 2,000 new fiction words a day while also leaving time for blogs like this one and/or magazine articles. What's 2,000 words a day equate to? Approximately one new novel per month. That's a lot of books. My ability to do this day in and day out means that I've accomplished what I set out to do in writing school, when the profs were having a good belly laugh.

Proliferation is Profit but...

Just because I can, theoretically write one novel per month, doesn't mean I should be publishing one novel per month. Over the course of three years, I've published maybe thirty products, most of them under my own imprint, Bear Media, and some of them with publishers likes of Down & Out Books, Polis Books, and other publishers (I'm what they call a hybrid author). My belief was that the more content the better. That might hold true for the romance genre, but as it turns out, it doesn't necessarily hold true for the crime, hard-boiled mystery, and thriller genres.

Flooding the Market

I believe at present there's something like sixty million books available online. You might ask yourself, How the hell can I compete? The market is flooded. But I firmly believe that I'm only competing against my own genre(s). Maybe there's far more thrillers available today than when I first started, but many of them are subpar or aren't really competition anyway. However, when I flood my own market with too much of my own work, I actually rob myself of royalties. Even if the Beatles had put out a new record every month for ten years, there would have come a time when they would have been stretched just a little too thin, and sales would have suffered. One must give one's readers (and listeners) a chance to keep up. One must give them a chance to breathe, or so I've discovered.

Proliferation to Profit Conclusion

After speaking candidly with one of my publishers, 2020 will usher in a new phase for me, in which I will only publish one full-length novel per quarter. This should give my readers both old and new, a chance to catch up with all of my published works. It doesn't mean I might not put out a novella or a short story or two in between, but full-length works will be released one once per quarter. That should make everyone happy, including my publishers and my wallet.

In this new golden era of writing and publishing, proliferation is extremely important if not necessary. But man was not made to eat a full meal, every hour on the hour. He was made to eat three squares per day. Anything beyond that, and you just make yourself sick.

6

5 Reasons Why I Don't Miss Marriage

A buddy of mine went through a nasty divorce last year. Almost every late afternoon I'd see him stumble into our local pub, his face pale, hair disheveled, eyes wide and bloodshot. In the words of the great Hemingway, he looked, "defeated." He'd sit beside me at the bar, order a beer, and practically start crying into it.

"She's taking me to the cleaners, Vin," he'd lament. "But I don't care. I just want out as fast as I can. I can't take it anymore. The fights, the tension, the no sex. She doesn't even do my laundry. Hasn't in years. But she expects me to pay for her personal trainer and her ski trips."

He was also in pain because the on-the-skids couple shared a teenage daughter, and my friend was naturally concerned about the child's well-being and her mental state while her parents were going through this horrid divorce.

Me, having been divorced twice before, the first one after a stormy nine year marriage and the second after only thirty-six months of a marriage that should never have happened in the first place, offered up the only words of wisdom I could.

"Just know this, my friend," I said. "As hard as things are now...no matter how emotionally draining all this is...no matter how much money you're losing...the time will come when you will wake up in your apartment on a Sunday morning. You will make the coffee, maybe bring it outside with you. Something will happen to you then. You will be surrounded by silence and peace, and for the first time in years, you will be alone, but you will be happy."

He took a big deep slug of his beer, wiped his mouth with the back of his hand, and said, "You really think so?"

"I know so," I said. "I've been divorced for 15 years, and truly, they have been the happiest years of my life."

It's true. My divorced years have been the happiest and most content of my life. I've solo traveled to more than 30+ countries, written and published thirty five novels and novellas, lived as a foreign correspondent part-time in Italy, dated a whole bunch of women, some a lot younger, some older. Taken road trips, hunted, fished, and gone to the bars whenever I wanted. I also enjoy my mornings, alone, writing at my writing desk or outside on a picnic table.

But what are the specific reasons I don't miss marriage? Here are five of them.

1. Money: There just never seemed to be enough of it. Even when I was doing my best, making more money than ever before, there was always a reason to bicker over the bank accounts. Either I wasn't bringing in enough from royalties, or her credit cards were maxed out. Maybe one of the vehicles needed major repairs, or the furnace blew, or she just insisted on a brand new king sized bed with the fancy headboard when the bed we had would suffice.

2. Fighting: Of course, the money thing leads to fighting. If you haven't been castrated like so many men are these days, you're going to stand up for what you believe in, and you're going to express your opinions, sometimes loudly. On occasion, dinner plates get tossed against the wall. One of my wives hauled off and punched me in the mouth. I stood there and took it like a man (we don't get to punch back, nor should we ever). Living in a constant state of siege can take a lot out of you. Sometimes you fight so much, you don't remember a time when you weren't fighting.

3. Sex: It's great at first. It might even be awesome. When you were still just dating, you did everything sexually possible in all sorts of strange and exciting places like on the kitchen table, or in the car. Once we did it on an airplane coming back from Europe. Those were the days, my friend. Things are still good when you're newlyweds, but eventually the luster fades and she finds inventive excuses to take the night or nights off. Eventually those nights off can turn into weeks and months off.

4. Boredom: You want to go out to bar and blow off some steam. She wants to sit at home and watch Grey's Anatomy on Netflix for hours and hours on end. You want to go for a hike. She's not up to it that day. How about skiing? She doesn't like to ski anymore. Fishing? Are you kidding me, I hate fishing. Sex...Don't even go there.

5. Freedom: To do whatever you want to do when you want to do it. Trust me when I say, this is the absolute worst part about being married. You just can't up and go where you want, when you want. You need to ask permission of sorts. What do your guy friends call it when you are able to meet them out for a beer on a rare Thursday night? You got yourself a kitchen pass. Most marriages end up in a sort of passive/aggressive tug of war, a struggle for ultimate control. My marriages were no exception. For going on a decade and a half now, I do whatever I want to do when I want to do it. Period. Full stop. Selfish? Maybe. But it's a short life. And it's entirely liberating knowing you can live your days and nights that way.

Okay, I know, some heads are blowing up right now. Some might even sense a bit of a misogynistic tone, which isn't the case at all. I love and respect women. I was raised mostly by women. I'm just speaking from personal experience. But I also sense you know what I'm saying here is more true than false.

This is not to say marriage isn't a sacred bond between two people who truly love one another until death do you part. Two people who deep down inside need one another like Lewis needed Martin, McCartney needed Lennon, and Hall needed Oates. Two people who are as much best friends as they are lovers and lifelong partners.

Perhaps I just never found that kind of love. Or perhaps, like my first wife (and now friend), said to me not long ago, "Vince, you're not marriage material." Like I've already admitted, I am a bit selfish and stubborn about doing things my way.

But I do know this. I did get back together with my second ex-wife some years back and we had a wonderful time traveling together to places like Rome, Florence, Venice, and Paris. We did lots of things together with our daughter. We were a solid unit again. Problem is, I wouldn't commit to marrying a second time, knowing in the back of my mind that she would likely divorce me a second time.

7

5 Reasons Why I Miss Marriage

In my last article I wrote about a man who'd gone through a horrible divorce last year. Me, having been twice divorced, offered him this sage, Dalai Lama like advice. One day, you will wake up in your new apartment and you will head outside with your morning coffee and experience a happiness and peace like never before. Very recently he told me this exact thing happened to him. He also thanked me for my words of wisdom, if you want to call them that.

Today, he has found a new love, and I'd wager the mortgage he's going to ask her to marry him one day. If he does, it will be his second marriage and one that will stick for him. Fingers crossed. I have seen them together and they are perfect for one another. She is his Yoko and he is her John. No question about it.

Will I ever get married again? My answer is a solid no. I've have my chances and once you're two and out, my guess is you've developed not bad luck, necessarily, but instead, a pattern of behavior. Marriage should not be chalked up to an anthropological experiment.

Do I enjoy my freedom to do whatever I want to do whenever I want to do it? I cherish it and I'm always going on about how wonderful the free life is. But are there aspects of marriage that I miss? I would be remiss if I didn't admit the truth. I do miss some of the wonderful things a good and solid marriage have to offer.

Here's five of them:

1. Stability: Living the life of the roving bachelor, while having its many advantages, can sometimes get old. You don't always eat right, or you

drink too much, or you develop bad habits like sleeping too late or too little. If you don't have a steady girlfriend, you sometimes serial date and that also gets wearing on the nerves. My second wife once said I was the type who always needed a girlfriend to get through the night. That's not entirely true since I spend most every night alone. But there's also some truth to it.

2. Friendship: The shame of my personal divorces are that I was good friends with both my wives prior to our getting married. Only when we were thrust into the responsibilities of what's intended to be domestic tranquility did things start to get ugly. At the risk of sounding like a broken record, I can be a little bit selfish about the things I want to do, when I want to do them. But I do miss opening a cold beer at the end of a long writing day and shooting the breeze with my ex while she made dinner for our daughter. We used to get along great, until other things got in the way.

3. Parenting: I'm going to admit something else, and I'm not proud of it. I'm not the best parent in the world. You won't see my ugly mug on the cover of Parent Magazine. Don't get me wrong, I love kids. If the situation with my second wife had been better, we might have had more than one child. Problem is, I loved the kids, but I wasn't a very good disciplinarian, and what's worse, if I thought a decision my wife made regarding the child wasn't the best, I'd rarely back her up. Marriage is a team effort and if you have one member undermining the other, things are going to fall apart. As a single man, I feel like I'm an even worse parent since I'm very much absent from one of my kid's lives. But I'm working on that.

4. Health: They say (you can Google it) that a married man lives a longer life than a single man. As an unmarried man for the past fifteen years, I can definitely see where this is the truth. Unmarried men tend to eat out more often than they should. We take chances we might

not otherwise take, like visiting war zones or places where revolution and/or terrorism are rampant. We are also lonelier than many married men. Even men who are in bad marriages aren't necessarily lonely. I love to travel solo, since I pretty much have no choice but to do it that way. Which means it's a special treat to actually travel with a wife or a girlfriend.

5. Days Off. I work all the time. That was one of my recent ex's problems with our relationship when we tried to make it work a second time. However, come Sunday, I would make sure I did not work at all. If I had my way, I'd gather up the troops and we'd head out on a day trip. Didn't matter where. The Catskills maybe, or simply an apple orchard to pick a few bushels. It was the being together part that meant the world to me. It's something I definitely miss about being married.

I doubt many heads are blowing up over this article. Because like I mentioned in my last piece, 5 Reasons Why I Don't Miss Marriage, I'm coming at you from personal experience. So I'll ask of myself the million dollar question one more time. Will I ever get married again?

The answer is still no. I do love my freedom too much for that. Naturally, if the perfect relationship presented itself, I would consider living with a woman. As for legal marriage, however, no dice.

But then, perhaps I had my chance to enjoy a good marriage for all its hardships and warts, and just blew it. Or maybe we both blew it at the same time. Sad thing is, we'll never know.

8

Tony Bourdain: Reflecting on the Writer/ Chef who had No Reservations about Anything

"Bullshit!"

Such was the first word rendered on the very first episode of Anthony Bourdain's 2005 culinary adventure cable TV program, No Reservations. Talk about hooked. I was head-over-heels for the show from that moment on. Or should I say, heels-over-head. As an adventure traveler who loved food, but didn't know much about preparing it, that's how much I loved it.

I'd known of the former top chef peripherally in crime lit circles in the mid-1990s since he used to write paperback mass market mysteries. He's even published at the same imprint as I am in Japan. It's possible if not probable I met him once or twice at an awards ceremony or publisher's dinner in NY (I was always running into Mario Batali. Super nice guy BTW) I never gave much thought to his day job as a cook, until his hugely successful 1999 memoir burst onto the scene, Kitchen Confidential, and entire generations of foodies stopped eating fish on Mondays due to its signature essay of the same title. It's a pisser, let me tell you.

Mine and my then wife, Laura's favorite NYC restaurant became Les Halles on the corner of 28th and Park, back when it was still a small bistro where you could get sweet breads, steak frit, eat at its small bar, and smoke cigarettes right outside the door and nobody gave a shit. The restaurant was expanded later on but it was never the same and more recently it has closed forever. That's sad enough, but to lose its chef forever...now that's disconcerting. But Bourdain would break the bonds of NYC to become something of a phenom. A culinary adventurer who, and I quote, "... will risk everything...I've got nothing to lose." That risk earned him millions of dollars and world adoration.

After all, back in the early 90's he was a heroin addict reduced to selling used CDs on the inner city streets for food and beer money. He had a love affair with alcohol which lasted up until the end. His favorite music was punk rock...New York bands like The Ramones, Patti Smith, Richard Hell and ummm, Suicide. He cut the sleeves off his black CBGBs t-shirt and he adored his Marlboro cigs so much that a chef bud of his invented a custard dish that featured the vague flavor of a Marlboro Red cigarette. Yup, you can't make this shit up.

When he began his first low budget show, A Cook's Tour, back in the very early 2000s his heart was breaking while his long time partner and wife Nancy Putkowski and he were breaking up. Some of the early episodes demonstrates his desperation (he jumps off a cliff into the sea at one point). But he had a searing wit, wasn't afraid to call out his fellow Food Network culinary pros on being suckups or just plain sucking (he was particularly tough on Emerald and Rachael Rey...it pains me to even type the latter's name). After all, Tony was authentic. He was the real deal. He hated the commercialization of anything, especially when it came to food and words.

He would eventually inspire me as a writer, so much so that back in the mid-2000s I wrote a non-fiction proposal for a book called Construction Confidential, an insiders look at the building business (He, no doubt, would have laughed at it). It was rep'd by the William Morris Agency but went nowhere (Thank God!). Food is way more romantic and emotional than banging boards together or pouring a concrete footing.

But when I started traveling not occasionally, but often enough to lose yet another wife, Tony Bourdain was never far from my thoughts. I never travel without looking at his essays and videos first. Just last night I was once again YouTubing his many visits to Cambodia and his favorite place on God's earth, Vietnam. Here's a little taste of his foodie adventures in the 'Nam.

Last year I made my way to So. East Asia on a research trip for my novel, Tunnel Rats. The month-long excursion occurred not long after his suicide — a trip that included sleeping on the floor of a boiling hot wood shack over a rice paddy in Cambodia. Something Bourdain, ever the authentic, would have been proud of. I ended up dedicating more than a few cold beers and whiskey chasers to Tony. In truth, I was searching for his ghost to be bellied up to a bar right beside me. Thailand, Cambodia and Vietnam were not only his self-professed favorite places on earth, but they were also his idea of heaven.

Whenever a literary hero of mine dies by suicide it rattles me to my core. Brautigan and Hunter Thompson come to mind. And naturally, Hemingway. The late, Jim Harrison, another lit hero of mine who also considered suicide at one time over financial worries, said that when he saw his daughter's red bathrobe hanging on the doorknob, he knew that he couldn't go through with it.

The tragedy: Tony Bourdain leaves behind a little girl from his failed second marriage and that's the saddest thing of all. Jim Harrison, who was a gourmand in his own right, also added that the next meal is also worth waiting for.

Too bad Tony Bourdain didn't wait for one more great meal. And one more after that, and one more after that. Eventually, he might have changed his mind. Okay, maybe he would have changed his mind. Like another great writer who also took his own life during his middle-aged years once wrote, Isn't it pretty to think so.

9

How to Easily Create Convincing Characters

One major aspect of the craft that fiction writers seem to struggle over is creating convincing characters. I'm not blowing my own horn here when I say I don't have any trouble at all coming up with the personalities who inhabit my books, novellas, and stories. In fact, creating them is rather easy.

Why? Because they already exist.

There is simply no reason in the world to invent a main or supporting character out of thin air, especially when they exist all around you in the form of friends, family, and even enemies. It's this last group that especially intrigues me.

For obvious reasons, I'm not going to name names, but I have more than a few backstabbers and jerks who have made it into my books as bad guys and gals. And here's the best part, I believe they know who they are because I'm not shy about describing them to a T. They are a-holes in the books, and they are the last ones on earth who would ever want to admit they acted like an a-hole, so they never call me out on it. Of course, I don't use their real names, but on occasion, I might come close.

But are there any bad guys I can admit to having written about?

The crazy psycho dude who sucker-punched me in a bar in Italy a couple years back has made it in. I truly hope he's reading this, that is he's still alive and not floating in the Arno after pissing off the wrong guy or guys.

Another guy who made it into one of my novels was a young man who axe murdered his father and attempted to axe murder his mother. His name is Chris Porco and he lived my area. Google him.

Yet another character I wrote about is a guy who would notoriously demand the bartenders and servers at my favorite local to move mountains for his orders and get this, only tip them a penny or two, if that. Talk about a dick move. Yup, he made it into a novel.

Just the other day, a bicycle Nazi who lives in my old neighborhood nearly ran me over in the bicycle/jogging lane on the boulevard outside my home because, "This lane is for bikes only!" He's a total douche and guess what, he's earned a coveted spot in one of my books. Trust me when I say, it ain't gonna be pretty.

Some old loves have appeared in my books, but they are rarely bad characters since I always try to see the good in the life we shared together, even if it didn't work out. I always include good high school and college friends. Often times I use their real names, with their permission, of course. Or I might change a letter or two, just to make it legal. But I know these people in and out, so it's easy to write about them.

I've even gone so far as to use famous movie and television stars as characters. I definitely had Gerard Butler in mind when I wrote my newest thriller, The Girl Who Wasn't There.

So how do you go about writing convincing characters when you're taking them from people who exist in your life?

Use their real names in the first draft. Describe them exactly how they look today or how they appeared years ago. Maybe you know them well enough to age them a little.

In the second draft, you can change little things here and there, while improving on others. In doing so, you begin to make the characters all your own.

In final draft, change their names or, like I already said, keep the names if you know it won't cause you any legal hardship down the road.

All this is not to say I don't make characters up out of thin air. I do. But they are usually minor characters, some of them not even having names other than Stocky Man or Thin Young Lady, something like that.

If you want to create convincing characters easily and effectively, look no further than your friends and enemies. Oh, also don't be afraid to look into the mirror either. For you are by far your best invented leading man or woman.

10

20 Secrets to Living a Long, Happy Life

The oldest living male (according to Guinness World Records anyway) died not long before the pandemic. He was 112. His name was Bob Weighton, and from the photos I've seen of him, he seemed like the happiest man alive. His smile wasn't just a forced smile, but instead, a boyish, almost childish smile. There perhaps lies one of the secrets to a long and happy life. A life perhaps that extends well beyond the average lifespan of the American male or female.

While I haven't engaged in any sort of scientific study on the subject of long life, I've done enough reading and YouTube cruising to come to a few conclusions of my own. Here are just a few secrets to living longer, healthier, and happier (they are presented in no special order of importance).

1. Find a real purpose in life. If you're going through the motions of a job day after day, month after month, year after year, you're dying inside just a little bit everyday. Find your true purpose in life and follow it passionately.

2. Find true love. Even if you married and realized after a number of years, the person lying beside you in bed night after night is not the right one for you, it's okay to end it, then venture out and find your true love. You only go around once. Sharing it with the right partner can add precious, happy years to your life.

3. Moderation. Eat well, but don't gorge. Drink well, but don't get drunk. Good food and drink are two of my greatest passions, and although I imbibe on a daily basis, I try not to engage in abuse. Eating

the foods you love and drinking alcohol is not a right, it is a privilege. It brings pleasure and happiness to life. Why would you want to suddenly have to give it up?

4. Travel. Going to foreign, sometimes exotic destinations expands the mind and the heart. When you're sitting in a hot, Asian, open air restaurant in 100 degree heat and 90% humidity, the sweat pouring off your forehead while you eat greens covered in red ants, and washing it down with a local beer, you know you're doing something special. You're making memories that will not only enhance your life but extend it.

5. Don't sweat the small stuff. Let's face it, money comes and money goes. Relationships begin, and relationships end. Bills sometimes pile up and sometimes they get paid. The plane is delayed, the Jeep needs new tires, and the US Congress can't get its act together over anything. Just brush this stuff off, like water off a duck's back.

6. Take a huge dump, daily. Hey, it's a fact of life. We all got go sometime. I've done some of my best work in a toilet tent set up on the banks of the Ganges where we were camping out in India and also in a hut in the Atlas Mountains of Morocco. Taking a healthy poop is not only crucial for cancer prevention, it makes you feel good. I know too many people who are so pent up, angry, and frustrated all the time they can't hope for any kind of regularity without gallons of Metamucil. And even then, they can't go. Curiously a lot of these people are wealthy.

7. Exercise daily. I run and lift for two hours everyday. I also walk a couple of miles on top of it. It not only keeps me in top physical shape, it keeps my mind in shape as well. Constant endorphin release is nature's crack, and it's a life enhancer.

8. Don't smoke. I used to smoke, especially when I was drinking beer. Then, one day fifteen years ago a little voice in my head told me if I had even one more cigarette, my life would be cut short. I listened to the voice and never smoked again.

9. Have sex (a lot). Let's face it, there's nothing that feels quite so good as getting lai...Oops, sorry, this is supposed to be rated G. Let me start over. There's nothing that feels quite so good as engaging in safe, consensual physical relations with a loved one (or two if you're so inclined). It's passionate, fun, romantic, and it can be memorable or even funny at times (Once upon a time, my partner and I started laughing hysterically in the middle of you know what, and it remains a wonderful memory). In the end, sex is a life saver (except for former NY Governor Nelson Rockefeller who is said to have died while whooping it up with his GF).

10. Laugh it up. Come on, do I need to explain this one? Laughter is the best (fill in the blank _______________).

11. Take naps and sleep like a dog. I take a nap every day, or most days unless I'm adventuring. I also try and sleep eight hours minimum per night. Sleep deprivation is considered a torture in many countries. Getting the proper amount will prevent you from getting run down which can lead to sickness and perhaps even lead to heart disease and/or cancer. Take a cue from your dog who loves to curl up on the couch and sleep the day away. When they wake up, they love to play.

12. Read. Reading is one of the greatest pleasures known to mankind. For me, every book I read is an escape to another world. It's travel without having to foot the bill for the plane and the hotel.

13. Live simply. I don't need a big house in the burbs, or three vehicles in the driveway or a country club, or anything that requires a ton of money along with my time and attention. I can live on $30K per year as

easily as $300K per year. I've done both. I rent, I own my Jeep outright, I fish, I ski, I work out, I write, and I travel. That's about the extent of it and I love it.

14. Have children. No matter how long you end up living you will leave a great legacy by having kids. I want them to be with me when the time comes to check out. Norman Mailer had a drink with his many kids on the night of his demise. What a great way to go.

15. Don't hold grudges. Got exes out there? Paying child support? Still pissed off that she or he cheated on you? Or maybe you got fired or dropped from a publisher. The past is the past. You can't ever recover the water that has already run the course of a river, but you can concentrate on the water that's flowing right in front of you. Let go of the past, learn to appreciate the present, and the good memories you had with someone or something, and move on.

16. Get rid of negative influences and bad friends. If a friend or even a family member is constantly berating and/or judging you, it's time to set them free. They will cause you undo stress, and stress shortens the life.

17. Believe in God. Why not believe? The alternative is to believe in nothing, and nothing is a dark place.

18. Believe in Karma. Hey, what goes around comes around. You can create good karma for yourself or bad karma. It's your choice. Which leads me to...

19. Be nice. You will be rewarded with many friends and opportunities just by being nice. You can be tough when you have to but try and be as nice as possible. I am the first to admit, on occasion I've been a jerk in the past. That said, being nice is something I am constantly working on.

20. Have hopes and dreams no matter your age. I still feel like I'm just getting started as a writer and I'm in my mid-50s. I actually feel like a kid sometimes. There are so many places I want to go, so many things I want to experience. Like my dad used to say when he was in his 70s, "I'm a work in progress."

If life seems like a chore, you're going about it all wrong. If the time seems like it's flying, chances are you're doing something right. Seek out the things that make you happy. Learn to play. Learn to appreciate your health while you've got it. Like one of my good friends always says, "Life's good." So don't blow it.

What about you? What are the things you can do to add years and happiness to your life? What changes do you want to make starting today? Starting right this very second.

11

A Big Backlist is Your Frontlist...Really!

Over the course of my twenty-year career in professional publishing, if there's one thing I've learned, it's never what you've done or accomplished, it's always what you're about to do that's important. Publishers big and small, are always looking for the next big thing, the next big book, the next bigger than God author who is going to break out and amass great wealth for publisher's bank accounts.

And every year there is usually one writer who fits this bill. Almost always, the publisher creates the myth of the next big thing by tossing a huge advance at the poor soul (he doesn't realize he's a poor soul yet because he will of course be broke and needs the money badly), and the press will greedily snatch up news of the sale, the rationale being, if the book is worth so much money, it's got to be great!

Problem is, most writers don't earn out their advances, even humble ones. I was one of those mega six figure advance debut authors once upon a time and it nearly cost me my career in the short run when the six month bottom line turned out to be redder than Rudolf's nose. That's right, not six years, but six months. But for publishers, the point is not necessarily an author earning out a big advance right away as it is creating a buzz over something new. A book that is so fresh and unique it somehow deserves our utmost attention. Attention should, theoretically speaking, translate into sales.

But what about an author's backlist?

According to a recent essay by marketing genius Seth Godin, the aptly misnamed backlist is really the true money maker for both author and publisher. These are the books that sell perpetually for both author and publisher year after year after year. Yet, according to Godin, publishers only invest about 2% of their annual marketing budgets to any given author's backlist and the rest goes to someone or something that's new, and never been done before. Thus the old conundrum, it's never what you've done, but what you're going to do.

Another thing I've learned about publishing is that publishers, and especially their marketing departments, tend to think short term. If they don't think a book will sell well out of the gate, no matter its merits, it's rejected. These days a book has to conform to the algorithms established by the computer software or it's "Thanks but no thanks." Problem with this philosophy is that some books take time to sell.

That debut novel for which I received the mega advance, The Innocent? It didn't take off until a decade later when, for some inexplicable reason, it sold more than 100K+ copies in a matter of a couple of months. By then another publisher had bought it, and then yet a third publisher snatched it up along with the offer of a rather generous advance.

But how can that be?

The Innocent, as a viable book project was done, over, roadkill, six-feet-under, washed up, "You had your chance, kid, now beat it." You get the picture. Yet the book defied publisher (and marketing department) logic and suddenly took off. There was no rhyme or reason to it.

Eventually all my books become backlist books.

It only takes a few months these days for a book to be considered old. A fruit fly has a longer life than a new novel, no matter what the advance. Bookstores, the ones that are left standing, only have so much space (although indie bookstores that sell coffee and toys are on the rise). But thanks to ebooks and downloadable audio books, backlist books can now be promoted right up front with an author's new releases.

A few independent minded publishers see the value of actively promoting backlist books. One imprint in particular continually promoted The Remains even though it was released in late 2012. It once sold tens of thousands of copies per year, and during one year in particular, hundreds of thousands.

Because of that, I just published The Ashes, the novel's sequel and next year I'll publish the third book in what's become The Rebecca Underhill trilogy. I'm not looking forward to the follow up books to The Remains being frontlist hits (although that would be nice), but what I'm aiming at are those existing fans and future fans of The Remains who will be wanting more of the story. Those are the readers who will gravitate to the next two books in the trilogy.

It dawned on me recently...wait, scratch that...allow me to rephrase. The realization hit me over the head like a sledgehammer the other day while I was banging out a news story, that as a freelance writer and journalist, we only get paid for our time and once the story is published it's already old news. In other words, like that brand spanking new car you just shelled out thousands for, once you drive it off the lot, it's immediately lost both its original luster and it's top worth. And even that freelance payment has become so reduced thanks to free media outlets (like this one), that it's becoming harder and harder to justify the freelance writer occupation. It just doesn't freakin' pay anymore.

But by publishing more and more novels, novellas, and stories...by creating a backlist that's masked as your frontlist...you can create the gift that keeps on giving. Some books will appear to sell poorly out of the gate but that given time will grow into steady sellers. Some books will kill it out of the gate and then die a slow death. That is, until you repackage it and republish it, thereby breathing new life into it. And other books will sell respectably well out of the gate and sell steadily for the rest of your days, your children's days and their children's days and so on and so forth.

As a hybrid author, I can state with confidence that the writing business has finally become an occupation that's not necessarily concerned with what I'm going to do, but a hell of a lot more focused on what I've already accomplished.

For me, the past is indeed prologue.

12

5 Reasons You Should Quit Your Job Today if You've Always Dreamed About Becoming a Full-time Writer

For years you've dreamed about being a writer. Not just a guy or gal who scribbles a few lines here and there on your own time, or maybe writes a couple short stories per year and submits them to the academic magazines in the hope against hope that it will be accepted for publication. Instead, you've dreamed big.

You've imagined yourself living the laptop lifestyle of writing your Great American Novel while living nowhere near America at all, but instead, Paris, Rome, or maybe Casablanca (the French Quarter is particularly nice). You see yourself as a prolific writer, if only you had the time. You'd not only write novels, but articles, blogs, journalism, and even poetry. No matter what form the written word takes, you would embrace it.

Instead, you have a mortgage around your neck, kids underfoot, and a spouse who is presently not working. You feel more trapped than ever, because we're living in a time of pandemic and severe unemployment. Friends and family tell you you're one of the lucky ones. You still have a job, and you're still bringing in a guaranteed income. Why in God's name would you decide to pack it in now????

The Covid-19 epidemic has changed the world in ways we never would have thought possible just a few months ago. Even when a vaccine is finally created (and this can take a year or more), chances are the world will never go back to the old normal. Which is all the more reason you might consider leaving your old job today, especially if you've always dreamed about becoming a full-time writer. Here are five good reasons why you might want to finally make the move:

1. Your job may not be as secure as you think. With Federal Enhanced Unemployment already run out, and people strapped for cash, the economy which, thus far, has survived on stimulus packages, is bound to fail even worse than it already has. Even if another package is passed, and it will be, this too shall end, and we will be right back where we were before. Broke and in severe debt. Doesn't matter who is elected President in November. The country is up for some hard times.

2. The dollar is weakening at an almost catastrophic rate while inflation is already skyrocketing. Chances are your salary hasn't improved all that much over the course of the past ten years. Yet in that time, the dollar has lost at least $0.17 of its value. And that was pre-Covid; pre-over printing of money by the Fed. If you keep your job, it's good bet you will not only have trouble paying for basic goods like groceries and heating oil in the winter, but you will go through your savings too. That is, you have a savings.

3. The workplace is changing. We're working at home suddenly. We're having meetings via Zoom and/or Facebook Live. We have more time to educate ourselves on all sorts of topics by watching YouTube videos. Which leads me to this. You might want to become a full-time writer, but you're also wondering how you go about it. Just go to YouTube and seek the answer out. Here's a particularly poignant video on the subject.

4. Don't worry about becoming a traditional Query and Wait writer when you're starting out. If there's one thing in the literary world that's taking a huge beating during this new Covid era and what will surely become the Post Covid era, it's that the traditional publishing gatekeepers in New York City are going to take an even bigger financial hit than they have over the course of the last decade prior to the

introduction of the eBook and the streaming audio book. While eBook sales had been stagnating over the past few years, sales are up 20% just over the past few months. Makes sense too since people are not only looking for more and more ways to pass the time, they are looking for cheap entertainment. The eBook and the audio book fits that bill quite nicely. That said, think about starting a fiction and/or a nonfiction series and publishing it right away on an eBook publishing platform. Not sure how to go about it? YouTube it. It's far easier than you think. One caveat: Don't cheat on the process. Make sure you hire a very good editor and cover designer. Here's the key: If you have a novel or nonfiction book that breaks out and sells tens of thousands of copies an agent will contact you and land you a book deal (This is precisely what happened to my novel in my Jack "Keeper" Marconi series, The Innocent and also my bestselling stand-alone psychological thriller, The Remains).

5. Don't just write for the eBook publishing platforms. Write for Medium. Go to ProBlogger and seek out blogging jobs in your particular area of expertise. What expertise you ask? You just spent most of your life working a job you disliked or at the very least, wanted to break away from. Whether you like it or not, you're an expert in that area. Set up an account on Upwork and other sites like it and bid for thousands of writing jobs. I haven't sought this opportunity out but I know plenty of writers who do. But don't take my word for it. Just YouTube the subject "How to become a full-time freelance writer in 2020." Here's another video you might like:

I know what you're thinking. All this is easier said than done. But at the very least, why not begin the process while you still have your job, and then assign yourself a quit deadline. In other words, assuming you still have your day job a year from now, you will have written your first two or three novels and published them in eBook, written dozens of articles for Medium, established a couple or three clients on Upwork, and begun the process of creating an income separate from the job. You might not have replaced your regular salary yet, but if the worst happens, and the boss informs you, you no longer have a future at the firm, you are at least on your way to living the laptop life.

Writing full-time. It's what you've always dreamed about. These days, those dreams might not become a reality because you want them to be reality. But because you need them to be reality.

13

It Isn't Always Easy Being a Writer Even if You're World Famous

Bookbaby recently published an article detailing the trials and tribulations of some world-famous authors. Authors whom one would assume lived carefree lives of riches and unimpeded success.

But did you know Herman Melville's career was destroyed by a shoddy editing? Apparently, Moby Dick was butchered by its English editor, with whole sections being moved around, and some being excised altogether since they were deemed politically incorrect (I kid you not) or just unnecessary.

These edits happened without Melville's permission which was common in the mid-1800s. In the end, Moby Dick was so poorly received it only sold about 3K copies during the writer's lifetime, and up until that book, Melville had been a popular full-time writer. Poor guy had no choice but to take a job on the New York City docks prior to his death in 1891.

Back in the late 1800s, Mark Twain or Samuel Clemens or whatever you want to call him, put close to $200K into a automated printing machine that went absolutely nowhere. Think about it. That's the equivalent of more than five million in today's money.

To make matters even worse, his then business partner pretty much took the money and ran off. It busted the "Huck Finn" writer financially and in order to make up the cash, he embarked on a world tour which ended in tragedy when his daughter, Suzy, died back in the states.

Great Gatsby author, Scott Fitzgerald, suffered greatly from acute alcoholism. From one account, he drank a case of beer and a big bottle of gin every day for years and years. He also smoked like a chimney. His wife Zelda was a renowned loon and jealous of her husband's talent and the attention it afforded him, often making his domestic life miserable (no wonder he drank all that booze).

She eventually went insane (she was most likely severely bipolar) and he had her institutionalized. His readership dried up as the Depression era hit and no one wanted to read about wealthy upper crust types. He went to Hollywood to make some money there and drank his profits away.

Eventually he would write a series of "crackup" articles for Esquire I believe. Hemingway called them humiliating. He also said of Fitzgerald, his one time Parisian friend, "Poor Scoot, he confused growing up with growing old." The final check Fitz received from his publisher Scribners prior to the massive heart attack that killed him in 1940 was for $13.13.

Speaking of Hemingway, while he was arguably the most celebrated author of the 20th century, he was haunted by what he called the "black ass," or what you and I might refer to as severe and recurring non-psychotic depression. It ran in his family — a family which has been plagued by suicides.

On a physical level, it's also possible he inherited hemochromatosis, which is the premature hardening of the arteries. One who is afflicted with this disease should not drink alcohol since booze causes high blood pressure, which also results in hardening of the arteries. But Papa Hemingway was as renowned for his liquor intake as he was his words and adventurous, rugged individualist lifestyle. He should have died in one of the two plane crashes he was involved in in East Africa in the early 1950s. But he died the same way his father went out. By a self-inflicted gunshot wound to the head just a few days shy of his 62 birthday.

Ian Fleming drank and smoked so much, he died at the relatively young age of 56. Sylvia Plath committed suicide at 30. Truman Capote drank and drugged himself into an early grave. As as for Dr. Hunter Thompson? He ate a pistol barrel at his kitchen writing desk and blew his cranial cap away.

Okay, so this isn't the most encouraging of articles, especially if you not only want to be a famous writer, but you wish to emulate some of your heroes in the process. Just realize, even the most world famous and talented of authors have had their fair share of trouble in both the writing and the writing life. Chances are, you will too.

14

So, is it possible to earn a living writing fiction?

Probably not if you set out to write literary fiction (I recall one of my assigned reads back in MFA writing school was The Lime Twig by John Hawkes. I nearly barfed it was so boring). Literary authors, in my mind at least, view a commercially successful book as a failure, which is why so many literary writers must teach to make a living.

It's different for a genre author. We write books for the masses and gladly take their casheshe for our efforts and in the end, much of our work stands up to the test of fine literature anyway. But I'm getting ahead of my skis here.

The Experiment

This past year three years were more or less an experiment precipitated by my having been suddenly fired (after a corporate buyout, figure) from the one steady trade journalism gig I had going. For ten plus years it brought in a nice baseline income so that I didn't have to worry so much about royalties and/or advances. Plus I loved the gig. Don't get me wrong, I absolutely needed the book royalties if I was going to survive financially. It's just that because I enjoyed a writing/editing income separate from the fiction, I didn't wake up suddenly in the middle of the night wondering what I could be doing to sell more books.

When that long-term freelance gig suddenly vanished, I found myself with a choice. I could either look for more journalism-freelance writing gigs, or I could concentrate entirely on my fiction efforts and hope that I brought in enough money to at least keep the cable TV on.

Work, work, work

It turned out to be the most productive three years in my twenty-year professional writing career. I wrote at least 20 60K+ word novels, a couple novellas, and several short stories. In fact, I wrote and published so much stuff that if I write not a single word this year, I am all set for publishing (both indie and traditional) well into 2022.

How did I do it? Simple. I dragged my ass out of bed every Monday morning and set it in the writing chair just like any other working stiff. I wrote whether I wanted to or not (In all candor, I pretended to be an employee of say FOX, and they were expecting me to put out at least one novella per month, or no pay check. The ruse worked!).

Dollars and cents

Ok, so in terms of dollars and cents, what does all this mean? I'm not going to be entirely transparent here but according to the tax documents I've received thus far, I made a solid mid-five-figures all three years. In terms of past years, it wasn't all that great, but this is the nature of the business. Some years you're hitting home runs and scoring major deals and you're pulling in a comfortable six figures whether you like it or not. Other years are down years. Production years I call them. Years when you're working your tail off and not a whole lot is coming in, but the important thing is you're making a living.

A smart move

For once in my life, I made a smart move: Every advance I received (and I took in quite a few of them) over the past eight years from agented deals, I invested in mutual funds, which means those monies are working for me on a monthly basis. I also buy Gold and Bitcoin.

Another smart thing I did was to invest a big portion of my royalties into my indie books. When you invest in creating a new book, it's almost as if you're buying real estate. Eventually the return on investment will be enough to pay back what you spent and earn you a nice 10–20% per year of passive income from that point on. The key, is to write more quality books in a long tail series (like my Chase Baker action/adventure series) that will stand the test of time.

Steady growth

2017–2020 proved to be an interesting experiment. There were no big advances (I did receive four small mid-four-figure advances from two publishers), maybe five or six big Book Bubs, and maybe five or six titles that entered into the Top 100 (I'm doing this off the top of my head, but you get the point). Like I've intuited in previous posts, it was 36 months of steady growth, steady writing, steady sales. And in the end, I earned enough to make a living. I'm actually quite shocked, to be honest. If this were the old days and hybrid authorship were an impossible dream, I would have found myself begging for a job ("Welcome to McDonald's, can I take your order?").

Instead, I'm able to do something most writers only dream about. I can get up every morning, sit myself down at my laptop in my PJs, and write my particular brand of thriller and hard-boiled detective fiction. Hopefully my books are more interesting than the Lime Twig (No offense, Mr. Hawkes). And hopefully they keep on selling so I can continue to work at the only job there is for me.

15

Five Signs that Prove You're a Writing Addict

It's become a real problem. I've lost all control. For the longest time, I thought I could keep it in check, curb the craving, rein in my urges. But like all addictions, once it has its tentacles wrapped around you, it just begins to squeeze the resolve out of you more and more each day. It is stronger than you, cagier, more determined to have its way with both your mental and physical capabilities. If left entirely to its devices, it will reduce you to a wet bag of rags and bones. A slave to addiction is no way to go through life.

I began writing in earnest (that is, with the goal of becoming a professional) back in my mid-twenties. I woke up extra early every day before having to report to my day job as a construction worker and toiled away at short stories and articles. It was hard work and I truly sucked.

But all that changed with practice. Eventually I started getting published in the little journals and magazines. I even started working on a freelance and stringer basis for the local Times Union Newspaper. I was young, newly married, and an unstoppable writing machine, even if my work was still...well let's call it...unpolished. I was a neophyte filled with piss and vinegar and I was determined to become a successful professional writer. Perhaps, if I kept up the work ethic, I'd become an even more successful novelist.

I made my way to prestigious writing colonies like the Bread Loaf Writers Conference where I personally worked with Tim O'Brien of

The Things They Carried fame. Soon after, I was accepted into the Vermont College MFA in Writing program. It was there I started my first novel which I would finish soon after graduation. It was called As Catch Can (Now, The Innocent). My then agent sold the book in a high mid-six figures deal only a few months after graduation.

In a matter of 7 years, I'd gone from writing short stories in long hand on my dining room table inside my tiny bungalow to signing a two-book deal worth a quarter of a million dollars with a major publisher. I think it's safe to say if I hadn't become a writing addict by then, I'd definitely became one at that moment.

Hemingway once said he not only wanted to write as well as he could, but he wanted to do it better than anyone else had before him. That includes Shakespeare and Tolstoy. In the same breath, he also said that his drive to write was so strong, it was akin to an addiction. "An addiction is terrible," he added.

But how do you know if you're a writing addict? Here's a list of observations from my personal experience as a full-time novelist/ freelance writer that you might apply to your own life.

1. On my days off I write a blog. The late author Jim Harrison once wrote an essay about professional fishing guides down in Key West. They were so addicted to their sport that on their days off, what did they do? They went fishing, of course. If that doesn't make any sense, think of it this way. If you're used to jogging a couple of miles each day and for whatever reason (the weather perhaps), you're made to skip a day, you somehow don't feel right about yourself, physically or mentally. That, dear reader, is an addiction.

2. You forget to make money. The writing life, even for some of the most successful writers in the world, is not a very financially friendly occupation. If fact, it's not really an occupation at all, regardless of what

your tax return identifies you with. Sure, there are times you might have a solid six or even seven figures in the bank, and you think you're home free in terms of financial solvency. But then, we don't get a regular paycheck. It's not uncommon to go a year or two without earning anything at all. But you're so busy writing, you don't realize how much time has passed and suddenly, your bank account has diminished to the point of running on fumes. Just this morning I woke up, checked my account, and saw that I was $1,500 in the red. Oopsies! Luckily, I have enough savings to easily remedy that. Martha Gelhorn once write in her diary in the early 1950s that she'd only sold one short story that year and barely had the money to repair her new house much less take care of her adopted son. Her ex-husband, Ernest Hemingway, often had to borrow large sums from his publisher just to pay back taxes. Norman Mailer had to sell off parts of his Brooklyn townhouse to make up for terrible losses. Jim Harrison went bankrupt not once, but twice. More recently, the older brother of a renowned screenwriter who wrote one of the most popular movies of the late 1990s...a movie produced and directed by Spielberg...confided in me that not too long ago, his little bro had to use a credit card to pay his monthly mortgage payment. But none of these people were deterred in their ongoing quest to write the next big money maker. They are professionals after all and addicted to the writing life.

3. You've trained yourself to "write interestingly about a teabag." That quote comes from the freelance South African journalist Lizette Potgeiter with whom I worked at RT back in 2009–2011. She couldn't stress enough the importance of developing and fine tuning your craft so that you could make even the most mundane topics sound interesting. You want to survive as a freelance writer who actually pays his or her bills, you have no other choice.

4. You watch movies about famous writers. I'm a sucker for film that explore the writing life. Romantic dramas that revolve around

Hemingway are some of my favorite. His was a prodigious life of drinking, brawling, traveling, fishing, hunting, and divorcing, and all that stuff lends itself well to film. Because after all, nobody wants to just watch someone writing. It's all about watching the writer experiencing a unique life that then becomes vividly reflected in his work. Other movies about Ian Fleming are very interesting since he was a spy during World War II. He was the real James Bond. The two movies that portray Capote as he was struggling to write In Cold Blood are also favorites.

5. You're able to count the divorces and breakups on the fingers on both hands. Yup, as cliched as it might appear, I too have fallen for that one wrecked relationship after the other writer thing. Doesn't mean I didn't love the wives or the girlfriends or didn't appreciate them as human beings. It's just that, in their eyes, my writing all too often seemed to come first. I never thought of it like that, simply because I have lots of firsts in my life. My significant other, my kids, my God, my country, my work...For me, you can't sum up a life in linear terms. My life is more like an ambrosia of things that come first. In any case, I'm once again gifted with a great relationship and being that I'm not getting any younger, I'm going to do my best to make it work while still making writing a priority (Translation: while still being an addict).

There are of course, other things that will determine if you're addicted to writing or not. Like lack of sleep, or starting new projects before you're finished with the previous project (I'm guilty as sin of that one), or not eating healthily or at all for that matter, not exercising, etc. You get the picture by now.

If you are a professional, full-time writer, writing as well as you can, consistently, should be the most important thing in your life. But you shouldn't allow it to take complete control over every aspect of your existence. That's what an addiction does. That's what being a writeraholic is like. Like a great man once said, good writing is an addiction. And an addiction is a terrible thing.

16

Speed Does Not Kill if You're a Writer

Some authors swear by it.

I'm not talking the chemical version, though some authors (one of them that guy up in Maine who wrote The Shining), have admitted to swallowing speed to boost productivity levels. I'm talking about one's natural ability to write a lot of good to great content and do it fast, or faster than the average author who maybe puts out one book per year. Prolific is the word I'm going for here.

Don't write so much

In the past I've written about my former agents and/or editors who have asked me to slow down, take some time off, don't put out so much material...whatever. While they might have defended their position by going on to say that time off would be good for me, I now realize they were more or less watching out for their own best interests. Publishers and agents can't wrap their brains around high volume clients (My present agent loves that I write fast and continue to consistently put out quality material).

Pulp writers wrote and wrote and got rich

The writers of the Pulp generation (the 1920s-1960s) were able to write lots of words and do so everyday, day in and day out. Some of these authors made millions for their bank accounts. They weren't writing with speed necessarily, but their output was steady, consistent, and they did it knowing that the more good work they produced, the more they would get paid. Sound familiar?

Writing school discourages speed

Back in writing school, one of my profs wrote and published a novel in 1975, and never published again. I overheard another prof telling a fellow student, "I don't make any money from my writing. I train dogs for that." Yet another wrote only when he felt inspired and another told me to my face that in the course of his lifetime, maybe he would write five or six very good stories.

Huh?

I guess that's why these people were teaching. Not for love of the game, but for the payday. I've always made my money from putting words together (discounting my days in the construction business). It takes discipline and it takes speed. These were things that were not taught in writing school. If anything, writing school taught me to write slowly and in some cases, not at all.

Writing as exercise

Writing for me is like exercise. If I don't do it on a daily basis...if I don't work hard...I don't feel right. It's as if my soul left my body and went on vacation for a while. So I write, everyday. Many people think I'm fast. I'm not (I still type with two fingers, sometimes four). I'm just consistent. This isn't a hobby. It's my work. My livelihood.

Listen, if I listened to every agent or publisher out there who told me to slow down, I'd be broke. But then, there was a time not so long ago, prior to the indie revolution and hybrid publishing (I'm a hybrid guy, meaning I publish traditionally and indie), where I was dependent upon these same agents and publishers who told me to slow down. Take your time, they said. Meanwhile, they would maybe take months upon months going over one of my manuscripts.

If and only if, said manuscript was taken on by a publisher, it would then sit around for another year or more before pub date. My advance, even if it was large, would be quickly swallowed up by the agent, the tax man, and the daily bills, not to mention those pesky credit cards many of us writers had to live on while we're taking our time.

Independent writers

We were slaves prior to the indie revolution, at the mercy of the process. And the process, dear reader, was very, very, very slow. Death by a thousand cuts. Not anymore. Now I can write what I want, when I want, and as much as I want. I can put the material out there for the world and my readers can buy direct. Oh, and I get paid once a month. Doesn't mean I don't work with traditional publishers because I do. It's just that I'm not dependent on them anymore. I'm free. Independent. No longer at the mercy of others.

Speed, it doesn't kill after all.

It frees.

17

How to Live and Write in a Foreign Land (Part I)

For a long time now, fellow writers, especially newbies, have been asking me how to go about working as a foreign correspondent and/or how to go about writing for a living while overseas. The simplest answer I can give them of course, is to just do it. But short of beating the old Nike slogan to death, the answer is a bit more complicated than for which I give it credit.

The good news however is, as freelance writers and journalists, we can pretty much live where ever, however we want while working for ourselves and enjoying the cash rewards for our labors (But listen, if you're looking to get rich, better that you stay in the burbs and go to law school). Free is the key word here and if you're like me, and do not like the idea of being tied and bound to any one particular community or job, then the life of the freelance foreign correspondent/writer is the perfect palliative for the work-TV-bed syndrome.

But how exactly do you go about getting work and sustaining a life outside of your native land? Since there's a lot of ground to cover, I thought I'd break this essay up into parts, this being Part I.

Part I. Preparation

1. This is the soul-searching part. Take a good look in the mirror and ask yourself what precisely it is you want to do with your life. Do you seek the security of a 9-to-5 gig? Do you like the idea of getting married, buying a house, and settling down in the suburbs? Are you satisfied with a couple vacation weeks in the winter and maybe another

week in the summer? If you answer yes to these questions, than becoming a freelance foreign correspondent is definitely not for you.

2. Do you get fidgety standing in one place for too long? Do you not enjoy sitting down for long stretches in front of the television? Are you more prone to take a five mile run than head to the mall for some shopping? Do you find yourself fantasizing about seeing the Taj Mahal, or standing under the Eiffel Tower, or hiking through the South American jungle with spiders under foot and monkeys overhead? If the answer is yes to all these questions, you are already on your way to living and writing in a foreign land.

3. How are your relationships going? Do you find yourself crippled unless you have a boyfriend/girlfriend? Can't stand the lonely nights so much that you must always be in a relationship? We all get lonely. It's a part of life. I've been married twice and divorced twice and yes, I'm prone to loneliness. But in some ways, it's okay to seek out that loneliness. Loneliness creates an edge in your work which it might not otherwise have. After breaking up with Ingrid Bergman and spending a long, lonely stretch in Los Angeles, Robert Capa, a man who loved to surround himself with friends and women, found himself back out in the field in Turkey. He wrote. "I'm a newspaperman again...I sleep in strange hotels, read during the night...It's good to work. It's good to be lonely." Novelist/freelance journalist Martha Gelhorn, even after adopting her son, found herself desperately seeking out places in Italy, Africa, and Mexico for months at a time where she could write her stories and books in peace, while at the same time corresponding with her lovers and preparing herself for the inevitable heartbreak. As he turned sixty, Norman Mailer woke up one morning as his 9th child was about to be born, and he lamented to his 6th wife, "All I ever wanted to do was live in Paris for a year and write a novel." This is not to say you can't maintain a relationship while you travel the world and write, it's just that your partner had better be very special and very understanding

of your needs. You in turn must do the same for them. In the end, you should always travel as lightly as possible when living and writing overseas. This includes the lightest emotional load as well.

4. Finances. In the next part I'll discuss what kind of work is best for you. But for now, take a good honest look at your financial situation. If you're in debt up to your ears, the debtors are going to chase you down, even if you end up living in Kathmandu for a while. This is the digital age, and you're only a click away. If you're thinking that traveling abroad as a freelance writer is going to make you loads of cash, think again. More than likely, it will cost you money for a while. In fact, don't even think of buying a plane ticket unless you have enough cash to hold you over for three full months.

(To be continued...)

18

How to Live and Write in a Foreign Land (Part II)

It's early evening and impossibly dark outside. A darkness made all the richer by the city smog and the lack of electricity in this revolution-plagued country. Zandri is riding in the backseat of a van that also contains his driver, an impossibly thin and bearded middle-aged man with a perpetual smile, and a fixer, a young woman, newly graduated from the university but now forced to cover some of her face as mandated by the new government.

Seated beside him is a friend he's brought along as a second set of eyes in a place where admitting you are an American can get you beaten or at the very least, detained for questioning. Better to say you are from Canada which will almost always invoke the response from those asking, "Don't die Canada Dry!"

But these are tense, if not dangerous times while across a piece of desert in nearby Benghazi, several American diplomats were brutally murdered during an organized terrorist raid on the consulate only three weeks earlier on September 11. Driving back on the busy highway from a day spent in Giza at Zandri's request so he could research the pyramids for his upcoming novel, THE SHROUD KEY, a green, 1990s era Toyota pickup pulls up along side the white van.

The smiling driver grows noticeably nervous as the three men who fill the Toyota cab lock eyes on the van and its four inhabitants. The fixer gazes upon the bearded and dark-eyed men inside the Toyota but then quickly removes her gaze, choosing instead to focus on the night-time road. Her fear is palpable like the hot, humid air.

Zandri isn't liking this, and he says so to his friend Barry. Barry is a most trusted confidant, but he is also fearless. A self-described left-wing "radical," he came to Egypt not only to back the writer up should things get hairy, but to get a first-hand look at what was happening here post-Arab Spring and with the Muslim Brotherhood now in power. A power that comes not from the many new banners of martyrdom that paint the walls of downtown Cairo or that's evident in the burnt-out state department building on Tahrir Square, but in the eternally black barrels of the AK-47s they shoulder when walking the over-crowded city streets.

The truck isn't going away. The van driver, who is now visibly sweating, puts pedal to the metal and guns it. The Toyota picks up speed, matching the van's, but then suddenly makes a sharp 90-degree left turn, not only cutting off the van, but causing the driver to swerve left, forcing the vehicle into a roadside ditch.

The van comes to a crashing stop, cracking the windshield. Zandri lurches forward, slamming his forehead against the seat-back. The fixer is saved by her seat belt. Barry in lying on his side on the seat.

"Holy shit," he spits as the Toyota stops in the sandy no-man's land between the two opposing lanes of highway traffic. "Guess this is when they get out and blow us away."

I'm thinking the same thing, but I don't say a word, as the driver tries his damnedest to get the crashed van started back up. But it's stalled and won't start. Panic begins to set in while he turns the key and pumps the gas. The now flooded engine strains and spits, but won't catch fire.

Zandri eyes the Toyota driver as he opens the door, gets out. Even in the darkness, Zandri can see that he's wearing a traditional long robe.

The passengers get out, but for the most part they are blocked from Zandri's view. They are however, partially visible in the coming and going headlights. Frustrated and afraid, the van driver opens the door, gets out. He raises up his fist and begins to scream at the Toyota driver. Zandri has no way of comprehending every bit of Arabic being lobbed, but judging from the tone, it's not entirely friendly.

Then, just as suddenly, the driver gets back in, slams the door shut, prays to Allah above that he will be most merciful and caring and will he please just, please, please, please, allow the van to start back up. He turns the key and pumps the gas like the state of the lives and afterlives of his passengers depends upon it. And it does.

The van starts.

He crunches the gear shift into reverse, hits the gas, and toe-taps the clutch. The van spits sand and gravel as it backs up and out of the ditch, on coming traffic be damned all to hell. Motorbikes, cars, and trucks carrying crates of live chickens or small arms for the Brotherhood swerve past the van.

But the van driver doesn't care. He throws the shift in first, and peels on out, transporting his four passengers from a danger zone as fast as the van wheels can take them.

Maybe life as an international journalist or foreign correspondent isn't always this exciting, but it can have it moments. Whether it's getting stranded in the West African bush after your 4X4 has sunk into a swamp or getting chased on foot by a gangster on the streets of Moscow, or simply enjoying a coffee in a cafe in Rome or Paris, being a professional writer in a foreign land not only requires a hard-working ethic, but it also requires long hours of relatively uninteresting assignments. That is you want to make ends meet.

What kind of work is available for you as a stringer or writer? Here's a sample of what's out there.

— Blue chip news outlets like CNN, Fox, RT, BBC, and more, can be lucrative in terms of your portfolio, but jobs are hard to get since most of these international news organizations already have full-time correspondents embedded just about anywhere you go. I was able to secure an ongoing gig with RT at a time when they were open to giving me a column and taking on hard news stories from all over the world. But that opportunity suddenly came to a close when they decided to minimize their staff of freelancers and stick with their full-timers.

— Trade outlets. Trade magazines specializing in everything from home decor to concrete to construction vehicles can be a very lucrative bread and butter gigs for the freelancer. I've been lucky enough to secure great gigs from some of the architectural design and construction trades in the recent past before I decided to depend mostly on fiction. Most of these trades pay well and on time.

— Glossy Magazines/Newspapers. Publications that specialize in travel stories and/or features on wine and cuisine are always popular. I've written for many of these magazines over the course of my career.

Some writers make a living by writing for in-flight magazines alone. Of course, there are always many newspapers that are looking for travel stories, or features stories from a faraway land. I've also written and stringed for lots of newspapers. But be advised, if an area is already HOT with news, chances are the news outlets have already sent their full-time journos there to cover the stories. But if you are fleet of foot, try and anticipate where the next big stories are going to happen, and get there before the major media outlets set up camp. Your best bet for finding work? Go to Journalism Jobs or, if you are already a working professional with the clips to prove it, you might join a professional organization like the Society of Professional Journalists. I'm professional SPJ member and they are invaluable not only for assignment networking, but also if you find yourself locked up in a prison in Peru, they can help get you out.

— Other opportunities. As most of you know, I write thriller novels, so until recently, I divided my time up between journalism and fiction. These days, I make about 90% of my money from fiction royalties and advances, while journalism makes up the rest. That said, much of my traveling now is centered around research for upcoming novels. But those writers who don't pen fiction can find ways to supplement their journalism income by teaching English in a Foreign Land (TEFL), or simply bar tending or waiting tables. Of course, those who wish to avoid the non-writing jobs can always hope for a rich grandmother who is willing to send them some cash once a month.

NOTE!

One thing that's required of all writers who wish to work overseas is to develop a gut or what Ernest Hemingway, himself (and his very talented grandson, John Hemingway) a one-time freelance foreign correspondent, called a built-in shit detector.

It's the voice inside you that tells you to go left when all external indicators such as road signs say go right. It's the thing that tells you to stop when there's nothing to prevent you from going on. Case and point: A few years back, I was set to enter into Syria via Turkey at the precise location where about a dozen or more journalists have entered and have since been kidnapped and in some cases, beheaded and/or crucified by ISIS.

While I had my driver ready to go, I did not have a willing companion to join me as backup (Never enter into an area of armed conflict without a second set of eyes!). My shit detector spoke to me, and in the end, I decided not to enter into the civil war plagued area until I could find proper backup.

A couple of months ago I received a note from my fixer in the wake of the journalist beheadings saying he was glad we didn't go through with the Syria border crossing last Fall.

He couldn't live with himself had I been killed.

19

Go Minimalist and Gain the World

You gather a lot of stuff after living on this planet for 50+ years. Hundreds if not thousands of books. CDs. Vinyl albums. DVDs. Even VHS tapes from yesteryear. It all collects dust while for ages you convinced yourself that one day, you would once more pull out the old flip-top DVD machine and watch This Is Spinal Tap for the umpteenth time. Or was it Aliens?

I have clothing dating back to my college days. Okay, undergraduate days anyway. And as a writer, I have more plain notebooks and diaries filled with the crappiest writing ever seen. Why I insist on holding onto mounds and mounds of failed and/or incomplete manuscripts is beyond me. Maybe one day I'll actually sit down, read them, and find a brilliant nugget or two.

Not.

It's all crap and like all crap it all deserves to be flushed.

There are tax returns for the past twenty years, divorce papers, and newspaper stories that I wrote back in my mid-twenties. Year books and old telephone books. How many old cell phones and accompanying useless chargers can one grown man collect? Pots and pans that never get used, more forks and knives than I can possibly use, old dishtowels, chipped plates, and piles of plastic bags from the supermarket. Oh, and you should see the junk drawer that's filled not only with useless, well, junk, but also dozens of fortune cookies and plastic packets of duck sauce and hot mustard.

My drawers contain pairs of boxer shorts so old they have holes, and socks that don't match. Some t-shirts are torn, but for some reason, I just can't part with them. One of my old work boots split at the seam between the leather and the sole and yet they still sit on my floor, like the boot is magically going to repair itself.

I have three bikes that never get ridden, a television that doesn't get used, a microwave that looks like JFK's brain on the inside, and maybe six partial boxes of spaghetti.

A pile of old business cards that I have collected through the years from places like India, North Africa, China, and Peru, are scattered all over my desk. Am I ever really going to contact any of these people ever again?

There are old suitcases that will never get used since I prefer backpacks, and why must I hang onto old running shoes once they're worn out? My typewriter collection has grown into an obsession. But then, I also save my old laptops, even when it's impossible to turn them on.

It's all just a bunch of useless junk and it's driving me insane.

Recently, I started purging myself of a lot of this stuff. At first it was a difficult if not impossible thing to do. It was like giving up not inanimate objects, but actual bits and pieces of my life. It was as if I were tossing away memories, the same way you delete a file from your computer.

I packed up the books and began storing them in my mother's basement (I now read and listen to books on my smartphone). I gave my sons my free weights (I'm still going to use them however.) The old manuscripts got tossed. I'm ditching all the old clothing I no longer wear and giving away all the old CDs, DVDs and VHS tapes. The old cell phones are being deep-sixed. The TV, the couch, the tables and most of the chairs will go to my kids so that they too can hang onto them for God knows how long. The bikes will go to Goodwill.

It's all taking some time, but it's a positive experience for sure.

A funny thing happens when you begin to part with all the unnecessary junk. You begin to feel lighter. Suddenly, your more minimal world feels richer, more fuller, more optimistic. I guess there's profound irony in cleaning your slate.

Change is good. So is purging your life. You should try it sometime.

20

Major Mistake Getting Back Together with My Ex-Wife

Of course, the title to this one could also be Major Mistake Getting Back Together with your Ex-Husband, but then, I'm writing from my own POV. But like the title suggests, I did this very thing back in very late 2011. I started seeing my ex-wife again, much to the chagrin of some of my closest friends who warned me that it can only lead to disaster. What disaster? I thought. We still love each other and doesn't love conquer all?

THE BACKSTORY

For the purposes of her privacy, I will call my ex, Leslie. She was actually my second wife, and when we divorced back in 2005, I was sort of in a bad place in my life. My first publisher and I had parted ways, and I didn't really have any publishing prospects for the future. I wasn't even freelancing much, and the money just wasn't coming in like it had been when we first started seeing one another back in late 1999.

In the meantime, we'd gotten married, bought a huge house in the burbs, and had a baby daughter. With all this fiduciary pressure on me to provide, I started panic writing a novel hoping to God it would sell for big bucks. But I hadn't earned out most of a quarter million dollar advance from my first book deal. That meant none of the big pubs were interested in giving me more money, no matter how good my new novel was.

I was in a real bind, and I began to drink heavily. I turned inwards, hardly socialized, and in short, became a real hot mess. So, when Leslie decided to pack it in, I actually couldn't blame her one bit. In fact, the feeling was so mutual, I never asked her for my portion of the marital assets, which at the time amounted to $40K, and God knows I needed it (my lawyer actually declined to represent me further at the time because of this). We agreed to a very fair, if not overly fair child support payment, signed our papers, and later on that day, we had lunch together.

Leslie and I not only stayed friends, we stayed very close, both emotionally and, on occasion, intimately. It was around this time, that some of our closest friends started hinting that we would probably end up back together again. They compared us to Hank and Karen in Californication — the down and out writer always pining for his lost love and mom to their daughter.

Along with a new book deal, getting back together with Leslie was the one thing I hoped for. To one day be back with my entire family.

FLASH FORWARD A FEW YEARS

One of the more positive impacts Leslie's and my divorce had on me was this: I had no choice but to get my act together. Instead of concentrating on a major deal that wasn't about to come my way anytime soon, I chose to take a Mulligan on my career, and start over.

I began freelancing again, reporting for news outlets like RT, and writing construction/architectural trade journalism for outlets like Globalspec. I was also publishing short crime fiction in various online publications. Eventually I got my third novel published by a small press.

I was back to making a living as a writer and moving back up the ladder quickly. I also started spending most of the Fall months on writing retreat in Florence, Italy. I took assignments in West Africa, Turkey, England, France, Greece and the Greek islands, undertook research projects in Egypt, Morocco, China, Russia, and God knows where else. I was living the life of the global freelance correspondent and loving it.

When I went to Italy with my then girlfriend, an artist, Leslie got upset. She kept texting me while I was at the airport, and while I was in country, asking me who I was with? Why couldn't I just tell her who I was with in Italy? Leslie and I had been to Italy once before together, and I think she felt hurt that I would take someone else to Rome, Florence, and Venice.

But it was during this trip I learned that one of my old novels, As Catch Can, which my agent had gotten the rights back for and changed the title to, The Innocent, was rocketing up the Bestseller Charts. It would eventually hit number 2 behind the Lincoln Lawyer which was a major motion picture at the time, and stay in the top ten for many weeks. It would go on to sell more than 100K units in 5 weeks. I was astounded. So were the publishers, one of which offered me the lucrative deal I'd been seeking for years.

MY DAD DIES

Then tragedy stuck. My 76-year-old, very in shape, dad suddenly dropped dead from a massive coronary. It was a shock to everyone. I wasn't seeing anyone at the time, and neither was Leslie. But she did something rather strange. She immediately came to me, to comfort me in my time of need, and to be there for me throughout the entire funeral process.

Although I was living with my two sons at the time from my first marriage, she asked me to stay with her and our daughter (let's call her Anna). I stayed in Anna's room and it allowed me time on my own to think about the impact my dad had had on my life and how he would be missed.

Since my dad owned a construction business that needed to be shut down now that he was gone, I was promptly made president, and while I was working on my new book deal, my articles, and preparing for new overseas adventures, I oversaw the successful closure of the business. I was earning more money than I ever thought possible at the time, and what just a few years earlier had been Vincent the Hot Mess, now became Vincent the Got it Together Finally.

WE MAKE THE HUGEST MISTAKE OF OUR LIVES

Leslie and I start sleeping together again. We not only become lovers, we become an exclusive couple. It's strange because we're as close and in love as a couple can be and I'm still paying her my weekly child support. But the love was real. I could feel it, and others around us took notice of it.

"Things are as they should be now," Leslie said some months later.

Life was grand. I had Leslie back, I was an in-person dad to my daughter, my career was pumping, I was writing as well as ever, and still traveling on research jaunts to some of the most exotic locales on the planet. I planned trips to Italy and France with the girls. I even arranged an overnight train trip from Venice to Paris where we would spend the New Years, thinking Anna would really get a huge kick out of it. And she did.

We took long vacations in Cape Cod, Lake Placid, and California. Enjoyed many, many weekends in New York City, ice skating at Rockefeller Plaza, shopping, walking, eating, drinking. I was still working a lot, because that's the nature of a business that doesn't abide by the 9–5 workday schedule. But no one seemed to mind at the time. Or so I thought.

When Leslie insisted I give up my writing studio which was located in a nearby apartment complex in order to live with she and Anna full-time,

I was both overjoyed and skeptical. Our living arrangement had been working really well for a few years. We were still going strong. Maybe my moving in full-time would get on their nerves. After all, I live and work in the same place. I might be underfoot.

But Leslie, who was gifted a certain amount of cash each month from her parents (my parents were also very generous to me), wanted to be free of that, justifiably. But the only way that might happen is if I were to become the official head of the household.

Anxiety began to settle in. Could I afford such an arrangement on a writer's salary?

"What if I don't move in?" I asked one day while we were on a neighborhood walk together.

"Then we break up," she said. And she meant it.

I moved back in. Big mistake.

THINGS SLIDE DOWNHILL

While at first, things in the household went fine, I began to notice a change in Leslie, and not for the better. For instance, I would get up early, and since I didn't really have an office to work in, I used the dining room table for my writing desk. This would annoy her to no end.

Once, she got so angry with me, she threatened, "If I see your laptop on the dining room table again, I'm going to smash it against the wall."

Okay then, time to set up the writing studio in the basement. Which is exactly what I did. I hated it. It's tough to be inspired surrounded by four concrete walls. In the meantime, Leslie, who was having some personal financial trouble, asked me how I would feel if I could help her pay off a substantial credit card debt, plus her semi-annual property taxes. I was already paying out far more than I felt was fair, and having voiced my opinion about the matter, she became angry with me. There they were again, those pesky money issues that seem to plague most relationships.

At the same time, she started working on her body. She joined a gym along with a few of her girlfriends, lost a ton of weight (which she didn't need to do in my opinion) and sort of took on a new attitude. She was pushing fifty and she wanted to become a new woman at the same time. Okay, I was down with that so long as it made her happy. And at the time, I would have given anything just to see her smile again.

The fiftieth birthday arrived and the party I had been planning for her didn't go off as well as she would have hoped. To be honest, I don't know the first thing about planning a party other than buying booze and food, so in the end, she and her friends sort of pitched in to make it a success.

The following day, Leslie asked me never to throw her a party again.

TRAGEDY (AND IRONY) STRIKES AGAIN

Some months after the ill-fated party, Leslie's dad suddenly dies. It's a huge shock to the family. Leslie and Anna grieve terribly and while I try to console them both, they push me away. It's the strangest thing for me to experience, since Leslie was so good to me when my dad passed. Why wasn't I able to provide her with the same comfort?

From that point on, she sleeps in the guest bedroom, and refuses all sexual advances. I begin to suspect that perhaps she's having an affair. We're not married, so it's not like we'd be going through another divorce if that's the case. I ask her if she's seeing someone, perhaps someone from the gym, and she gets angry. How dare I ask such a question?

Some weeks after that, while giving me a lift to the train station (for yet another funeral, this one in Manhattan), she breaks up with me for the second time. Her exact words? "It took your father dying to get us back together. It took my father dying to break us up again." I will never forget those words.

I begged her to change her mind. But like an ugly spider hanging from the ceiling by a thick web, she wanted me gone.

THE UPSHOT

I gave Leslie what she wanted and moved out yet again, and while this time, I didn't have to start my entire life over, I did spend considerable time wondering what the hell had gone so wrong, so quickly. I knew she was going through a sort of sad, if not depressed period, but I never saw a breakup coming.

Didn't I treat her and my daughter like princesses? Didn't I take them on amazing trips, buy them all sorts of stuff? Hadn't I put a $15K deck on her house and helped her out with renovating the bathrooms? Didn't I make them laugh (or try and make them laugh anyway)? Didn't I tell them I loved them enough? Hug them enough? Didn't I just love being in their company?

Leslie had been there for me during some of the proudest moments of my life. Winning the ITW Thriller Award in New York City, winning the PWA Shamus Award, hitting the New York Times bestseller list in three different categories, hitting the USA Today list for 7 weeks, hitting the number one spot on the overall online bestseller list with The Remains, enjoying cocktail parties in New York with famous authors like Clive Cussler, Lee Child, and Scott Turow.

These were special moments I was only too happy to spend with Leslie and Anna. But it wasn't much later on I came to realize, that therein lies the big problem. When things calmed down, I asked Leslie what drove her away again. She said it wasn't an affair and I believed her. It was instead, my writing, my obsession with my work, my travels, heck, even my fly fishing. Even when I wasn't physically writing, she added, I was still absent. Absent as a partner and a father.

Other things were mentioned too, but the writing was the big culprit.

"But that's what I do for a living," I said. "I came into the relationship writing and traveling and I wasn't about to stop now that we were back together. It's what worked for me, for us."

But my work was something that didn't work for her.

IN THE END

Like I said at the beginning of this long piece, after our divorce, Leslie and I remained very close. Even when we were engaged in relationships with other people, she was usually the first person I texted with news of a new publication or a writing success, no matter how small or trivial. We weren't together, but we were still a family, sort of.

But now, we don't speak. We don't communicate whatsoever. My daughter doesn't talk to me, and even the simplest and benign text messages will go ignored. What had been some very special memories from our getting back together, have now become bitter-sweet recollections. I also can't help but think this: if Leslie and I hadn't made the decision to give the relationship a second go, we'd still be close, and my daughter and I would be even closer.

On the positive side of things, I harbor no ill will whatsoever towards Leslie. I love my daughter to death, and I believe she will one day come back around. Time, it might not heal all wounds, but it does add perspective. I honestly feel no guilt about the relationship because I firmly believe I treated Leslie as well as I was capable. Would I do a few things differently? Sure. But isn't a relationship always a work in progress?

I've found someone else now, and she is a very special woman and I suspect I will spend the rest of my life with her. Like me she is very independent and in all honesty, she doesn't need me at all. She's entirely self-sufficient. She's supportive of my work, my travels (although she was nervous about my going to Chernobyl last fall), and my lifestyle. We enjoy the same things — the running, the weightlifting, the skiing, the fly fishing, the trips, the drinks, and the food. She is a special woman, and I am gifted to have met her.

I still feel badly (but not guilty) over what happened with Leslie, and our second go round together. It was a time filled with good and bad. But it was a time I will never forget. A time that still haunts me in my dreams.

If you enjoyed this book, please check out THE HYBRID AUTHOR MINDSET. Or go to WWW.VINZANDRI.COM[1] to grab all of Vince's books and stories, and to grab your free novel MOONLIGHT FALLS[2].

Allow me to thank you ahead of time, for your honest review of this novel!

Winner of the 2015 PWA Shamus Award and the 2015 ITW Thriller Award for Best Original Paperback Novel for MOONLIGHT WEEPS, Vincent Zandri is the NEW YORK TIMES and USA TODAY bestselling author of more than 130 novels including THE REMAINS, THE EMBALMER, THE SHROUD KEY and NOTORIOUS MOONLIGHT. Zandri's list of domestic publishers include Delacorte, Dell, Down & Out Books, Thomas & Mercer, Polis Books, Blackstone Audio, and Tantor Media. An MFA in Writing graduate of Vermont College, Zandri's work is translated in the Dutch, Russian, French, Italian, Japanese, and Polish. Zandri was the subject of a major feature by the New York Times. He has also made appearances on Bloomberg TV and FOX news. In December 2014, Suspense Magazine named

---

1. https://d.docs.live.net/5472b0e563fe9cd9/Documents/WWW.VINZANDRI.COM

2. https://www.amazon.com/dp/B00S1XXMEY

Zandri's, THE SHROUD KEY, as one of the "Best Books of 2014." Recently, Suspense Magazine selected WHEN SHADOWS COME as one of the "Best Books of 2016". He was also nominated for the 2019 Derringer Award for Best Novelette. A freelance photo-journalist and the host of the popular YouTube Podcast, The Writer's Life, Zandri has written for Strategy Magazine, Living Ready Magazine, RT, New York Newsday, Hudson Valley Magazine, Writers Digest, The Times Union (Albany), Game & Fish Magazine, and many more. He also writes for Scalefluence. Zandri lives in Albany, New York and Florence, Italy. For more go to WWW.VINZANDRI.COM[3]

Published in the United States of America

The author is represented by Chip MacGregor of the MacGregor Literary Agency

Don't miss out!

Visit the website below and you can sign up to receive emails whenever Vincent Zandri publishes a new book. There's no charge and no obligation.

https://books2read.com/r/B-A-CQW-ZIQLC

BOOKS 2 READ

Connecting independent readers to independent writers.

Also by Vincent Zandri

A Chase Baker Thriller
Chase Baker and the Spear of Destiny

A Chase Baker Thriller No. 12
Chase Baker and the Lost Ark of God

A Chase Baker Thriller Series No. 3
Chase Baker and the God Boy

A Chase Baker Thriller Series No. 4
Chase Baker and the Lincoln Curse

A Chase Baker Thriller Series No. 6
Chase Baker and the Da Vinci Divinity

A Dick Moonlight PI Series
Moonlight Falls
Blue Moonlight
Moonlight Weeps

A Dick Moonlight PI Series Short
Moonlight Goes Viral
Moonlight Mafia
Moonlight Detour

A Dick Moonlight PI Thriller
Moonlight Falls: New and Lengthened Editor's Cut Edition

A Dick Moonlight Thriller Book 9
Dog Day Moonlight

A Gripping Ava "Spike" Harrison Thriller
The Concrete Pearl

A Gripping Dick Moonlight PI Thriller
Moonlight Sonata

A Gripping Tanya Teal Corporate War Chronicles Thriller
Primary Termination

A Jack "Keeper" Marconi PI Thriller Series
The Innocent
American Prison Break
The Jack "Keeper" Marconi PI Box Set

(A Keeper Marconi PI Thriller Book 5
Dressed to Kill

A Meta Man Time Travel Thriller
Meta Man
Meta Man: Mars 900 C
Cashless Bail
After Life

A Sam Savage Sky Marshal Thriller
Dead Heading
Tunnel Rats

A Short Thriller
Ghosts

Pembroke PInes
The Devil Won't Have You
The Girl in the Window
Go Get Me A Gun
The Left Hook
Autonomous
Delusional
Desperate Measures
Domestic Dispute
Living Doll

A Short Thriller Collection
Desperate Measures: A Short Thriller Collection

A Short True Crime Thriller
I Am God

A Steve Jobz PI Thriller
The Flower Man
The Extortionist

A Steve Jobz Thriller
The Embalmer

(A Thriller)

The Scream Catcher
Detonator

A Vincent Zandri Hard-Boiled Short Read
Bingo Night
Pathological

PULP Thrillers
Pulp 2: Three Gripping Thrillers Collected in One Box Set

The Handyman
Savage Sins: The Handyman, Season II, Episode III

The Handyman Season I, Episode I
Lust and Letters

(Vincent Zandri on Writing Book)
Pieces of Mind: Fictional Truths & Non-Fictional Lies about Writing
and the Writing Life

Writer's Life Volume 1
The Writer's Life

About the Author

"Vincent Zandri hails from the future." --The New York Times "Sensational . . . masterful . . . brilliant." --New York Post "Gritty, fast-paced, lyrical and haunting." --Harlan Coben, New York Times bestselling author of Six Years "Tough, stylish, heartbreaking." --Don Winslow, New York Times bestselling author of Savages and Cartel. Winner of the 2015 PWA Shamus Award and the 2015 ITW Thriller Award for Best Original Paperback Novel for MOONLIGHT WEEPS, Vincent Zandri is the NEW YORK TIMES, USA TODAY, and AMAZON KINDLE OVERALL NO.1 bestselling author of more than 60 novels and novellas including THE REMAINS, EVERYTHING BURNS, ORCHARD GROVE, THE SHROUD KEY and THE GIRL WHO WASN'T THERE. His list of domestic publishers include Delacorte, Dell, Down & Out Books, Thomas & Mercer, Polis Books, Suspense Publishing, Blackstone Audio, and Oceanview Publishing. An MFA in Writing graduate of Vermont College, his work is translated in the Dutch, Russian, French, Italian, and Japanese. Having sold close to 1 million editions of his books, Zandri has been the subject of major features by the New York Times, Publishers Weekly, and Business Insider. He has also made appearances on Bloomberg TV and the FOX News network. In December 2014, Suspense Magazine named Zandri's, THE SHROUD KEY, as one of the "Best Books of 2014." Suspense Magazine selected WHEN SHADOWS COME as one of the "Best Books of 2016". He was also a finalist for the 2019 Derringer Award for Best Novelette. A freelance photojournalist, freelance writer, and the author of the popular "lit blog," The Vincent Zandri Vox, Zandri has written for Living Ready Magazine, RT, New York Newsday, Hudson Valley Magazine, The Times Union (Albany), Game & Fish Magazine, CrimeReads, Altcoin Magazine, The Jerusalem Post, Market Business News, Duke University, Colgate University, and many more. He also writes for Scalefluence. An Active Member of MWA and ITW, he lives in New York and Florence, Italy. For more go to **VINZANDRI.COM**

Read more at https://www.vinzandri.com/.